Project Management Institute

THE STANDARD FOR PORTFOLIO MANAGEMENT

Second Edition

An American National Standard
ANSI/PMI 08-003-2008

The Standard for Portfolio Management—Second Edition

ISBN: 978-1-933890-53-1

Published by:
Project Management Institute, Inc.
14 Campus Boulevard
Newtown Square, Pennsylvania 19073-3299 USA.
Phone: +610-356-4600
Fax: +610-356-4647
E-mail: customercare@pmi.org
Internet: www.PMI.org

PMI Publications welcomes corrections and comments on its books. Please feel free to send comments on typographical, formatting, or other errors. Simply make a copy of the relevant page of the book, mark the error, and send it to: Book Editor, PMI Publications, 14 Campus Boulevard, Newtown Square, PA 19073-3299 USA.

To inquire about discounts for resale or educational purposes, please contact the PMI Book Service Center.

PMI Book Service Center
P.O. Box 932683, Atlanta, GA 31193-2683 USA
Phone: 1-866-276-4764 (within the U.S. or Canada) or +1-770-280-4129 (globally)
Fax: +1-770-280-4113
E-mail: book.orders@pmi.org

10 9 8 7 6 5 4 3

NOTICE

The Project Management Institute, Inc. (PMI) standards and guideline publications, of which the document contained herein is one, are developed through a voluntary consensus standards development process. This process brings together volunteers and/or seeks out the views of persons who have an interest in the topic covered by this publication. While PMI administers the process and establishes rules to promote fairness in the development of consensus, it does not write the document and it does not independently test, evaluate, or verify the accuracy or completeness of any information or the soundness of any judgments contained in its standards and guideline publications.

PMI disclaims liability for any personal injury, property or other damages of any nature whatsoever, whether special, indirect, consequential or compensatory, directly or indirectly resulting from the publication, use of application, or reliance on this document. PMI disclaims and makes no guaranty or warranty, expressed or implied, as to the accuracy or completeness of any information published herein, and disclaims and makes no warranty that the information in this document will fulfill any of your particular purposes or needs. PMI does not undertake to guarantee the performance of any individual manufacturer or seller's products or services by virtue of this standard or guide.

In publishing and making this document available, PMI is not undertaking to render professional or other services for or on behalf of any person or entity, nor is PMI undertaking to perform any duty owed by any person or entity to someone else. Anyone using this document should rely on his or her own independent judgment or, as appropriate, seek the advice of a competent professional in determining the exercise of reasonable care in any given circumstances. Information and other standards on the topic covered by this publication may be available from other sources, which the user may wish to consult for additional views or information not covered by this publication.

PMI has no power, nor does it undertake to police or enforce compliance with the contents of this document. PMI does not certify, test, or inspect products, designs, or installations for safety or health purposes. Any certification or other statement of compliance with any health or safety-related information in this document shall not be attributable to PMI and is solely the responsibility of the certifier or maker of the statement.

TABLE OF CONTENTS

LIST OF TABLES AND FIGURES

PREFACE TO THE SECOND EDITION

This document supersedes *The Standard for Portfolio Management*. The target audience for this standard includes: senior executives, management staff in charge of organizational strategy, portfolio managers, members of a strategic and/or portfolio management office, managers of program managers and project managers, customers and other stakeholders, functional managers and process owners with resources assigned to a portfolio, educators, consultants, trainers, and researchers. It remains of value to program managers, project managers, and other project team members, and members of a project or program management office. The standard is more tightly coupled to its companion standards: *A Guide to the Project Management Body of Knowledge (PMBOK® Guide)* – Fourth Edition, *The Standard for Program Management* – Second Edition and the *Organizational Project Management Maturity Model (OPM3®)* – Second Edition. While project and program management continue to focus on "doing work right", portfolio management maintains a concern with "doing the right work". In the time since its publication, the Project Management Institute (PMI) received hundreds of valuable recommendations for improvements to the *The Standard for Portfolio Management* that have been reviewed and, as appropriate, incorporated into the second edition.

As a result of those inputs and adoption of Portfolio Management processes, PMI volunteers prepared an updated version of *The Standard for Portfolio Management*. The project charter to update *The Standard for Portfolio Management* was to:

1. Revise the standard so that it would not conflict with any other PMI standards.

2. Ensure that the information contained in the standard was cohesive in concept and clear in writing style, and that terminology was well-defined and congruous with the other publications' terminology.

3. Research the way life cycles are currently being managed in portfolios and revise or expand them as necessary.

4. Examine the two Portfolio Management Process Groups and the nine portfolio management processes to determine whether combining, deleting, or adding new processes would add clarity to the standard.

5. Extend the standard to address knowledge areas relevant to portfolio management.

The major differences between the First Edition and Second Edition are summarized below:

1. All process names are in a verb–noun format.

2. A standard approach to discussing enterprise environmental factors and organizational process assets was employed.

3. Two Knowledge Areas were added to address Portfolio Governance and Risk Management.

The *Standard for Portfolio Management* – Second Edition extends the organization from the first edition and is organized into two sections:

Section I, The Portfolio Management Overview, Framework, and Processes provides a basis for understanding portfolio management. There are three chapters in this section.

Chapter 1, Introduction, presents a basis and purpose for the standard. It defines what a portfolio is and discusses portfolio management and the relationship between project, program, and portfolio management and presents an outline of the remaining document. The role of the portfolio manager is also discussed.

Chapter 2, Portfolio Management Overview and Organization, provides an overview of the process, describes stakeholder roles, and organization influences.

Chapter 3, Portfolio Management Processes, defines the two Process Groups: (a) Aligning and (b) Monitoring and Controlling. The processes are mapped to these Process Groups. Inputs and Outputs are also defined for each of the processes within the Process Groups.

Section II, The Portfolio Management Knowledge Areas, covers two Portfolio Management Knowledge Areas for Governance and Risk. There are two chapters in this section.

Chapter 4, Portfolio Governance, lists the processes and defines the inputs, tools and techniques, and outputs for this Knowledge area.

Chapter 5, Risk Management, lists the processes and defines the inputs, tools and techniques, and outputs.

Appendices

Glossary

The *Standard for Portfolio Management* Second Edition was presented in an exposure draft in early 2008. Many of the comments sent in by reviewers were incorporated into this edition.

SECTION I

THE PORTFOLIO MANAGEMENT OVERVIEW, FRAMEWORK, AND PROCESSES

Chapter 1

- Introduction

Chapter 2

- Portfolio Management Overview and Organization

CHAPTER 1

INTRODUCTION

This chapter defines several key terms and provides an overview of *The Standard for Portfolio Management* – Second Edition in the following major sections:

1.1 Purpose of *The Standard for Portfolio Management*

1.2 What is a Portfolio?

1.3 What is Portfolio Management?

1.4 The Link between Portfolio Management and Organization Governance

1.5 The Relationship Between Portfolio Management and Organizational Strategy

1.6 The Relationships Among Portfolio, Program, and Project Management

1.7 The Link Between Portfolio Management and Operations Management

1.8 Role of the Portfolio Manager

1.9 Portfolio Management Reporting and Metrics

1.1 Purpose of *The Standard for Portfolio Management*

The primary purpose of *The Standard for Portfolio Management* is to describe generally recognized good practices associated with portfolio management. "Generally recognized" means that the knowledge and practices described are applicable to most portfolios most of the time, and that there is widespread consensus about their value and usefulness. This standard is an expansion of and companion to information already provided in *A Guide to the Project Management Body of Knowledge* (*PMBOK® Guide*) – Fourth Edition, *The Standard for Program Management* – Second Edition, and the *Organizational Project Management Maturity Model* (*OPM3®*) – Second Edition. As a foundational reference, this standard is neither intended to be comprehensive nor all-inclusive.

This standard focuses on portfolio management as it relates to the disciplines of project and program management. Its application is intended for all types of organizations (i.e., profit, nonprofit, and government). When the term 'organization' is used here, it applies generally to these three types of organizations. If any portion of this standard typically is applicable to only a subset of these, the subset is identified.

In addition to the standards that establish guidelines for project management processes, tools, and techniques, the *Project Management Institute Code of Ethics and Professional Conduct,* guides practitioners of the profession of project management and describes the expectations practitioners have of themselves and others. The *Project Management Institute Code of Ethics and Professional Conduct* is specific about the basic obligation of responsibility, respect, fairness, and honesty. It requires that practitioners demonstrate a commitment to ethical and professional conduct. It carries the obligation to comply with laws, regulations, and organizational and professional policies. Since practitioners come from diverse backgrounds and cultures, the *Code of Ethics and Professional Conduct* applies globally. When dealing with any stakeholder, practitioners should be committed to honest and fair practices and respectful dealings. The *Project Management Institute Code of Ethics and Professional Conduct* is posted on the PMI website (http://www.pmi.org). Acceptance of the code is a requirement for the PMP® certification by PMI.

1.1.1 Audience for *The Standard for Portfolio Management*

This standard provides a foundational reference for anyone interested in managing a portfolio of projects and programs. This includes, but is not limited to:

- Senior executives making decisions about organization strategy,
- Management staff responsible for developing organization strategy or those making recommendations to senior executives,
- Portfolio managers, program managers, and project managers,
- Researchers analyzing portfolio management,
- Members of a portfolio or program management office,
- Managers of project and program managers,
- Members of a project, program, or portfolio management office,
- Consultants and other specialists in project, program, and portfolio management and related fields,
- Functional managers and process owners with resources in a portfolio,
- Customers and other stakeholders, and
- Educators teaching the management of portfolios and related subjects.

1.2 What is a Portfolio?

A portfolio is a collection of projects or programs and other work that are grouped together to facilitate effective management of that work to meet strategic business objectives. The projects or programs of the portfolio may not necessarily be interdependent or directly related (*PMBOK® Guide* – Fourth Edition). These components of a portfolio are quantifiable; that is, they can be measured, ranked, and prioritized.

A portfolio exists within an organization and it consists of a set of current components and planned or future initiatives. Therefore, portfolios are not temporary like projects or programs. An organization may have more than one portfolio, each addressing unique business areas or objectives. Proposed initiatives become part of the portfolio when they are identified, selected, and/or approved.

At any given moment, the portfolio represents a view of its selected components and reflects the strategic goals of the organization; however, specific projects or programs within the portfolio are not necessarily interdependent or directly related. By reflecting investments made or planned by an organization, portfolio management includes the processes for identifying the organizational priorities, making investment decisions, and allocating resources. Therefore, the portfolio represents the work *selected* to be done, but not necessarily the work that *should* be done. If a portfolio's components are not aligned to its organizational strategy, the organization can reasonably question why the work is being undertaken. Therefore, a portfolio is a true measure of an organization's intent, direction, and progress.

1.2.1 The Relationships Among Portfolios, Programs, and Projects

All components of a portfolio exhibit certain common features:

- They represent investments made or planned by the organization.

- They are aligned with the organization's strategic goals and objectives.

- They typically have some distinguishing features that permit the organization to group them for effective management.

- They are quantifiable and therefore can be measured, ranked, and prioritized.

Figure 1-1 illustrates the relationship of a portfolio and its components.

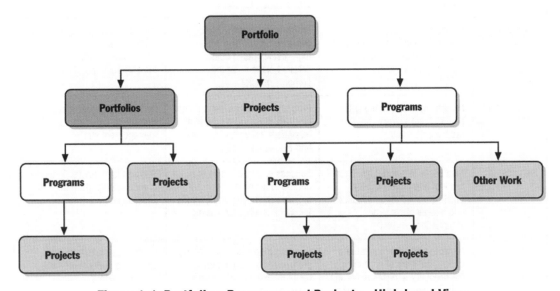

Figure 1-1. Portfolios, Programs and Projects - High Level View

Portfolio management ensures that interrelationships between programs and projects are identified and that resources (e.g., people, funding) are allocated in accordance with organizational priorities. Programs focus on achieving the benefits expected from the portfolio as determined by strategic organizational objectives. Projects are largely concerned with achieving specific deliverables that support specific organizational objectives.

The attributes of portfolio components can be further differentiated as represented in Table 1-1.

1.3 What Is Portfolio Management?

Portfolio management is the coordinated management of portfolio components to achieve specific organizational objectives. While this standard focuses on "project portfolio management," it is referred to throughout as simply "portfolio management."

Portfolio management is also an opportunity for a governing body to make decisions that control or influence the direction of a group of components (a subportfolio, program, projects, or other work) as they work to achieve specific outcomes. An organization uses the tools and techniques described in this standard to identify, select, prioritize, govern, monitor, and report the contributions of the components to, and their relative alignment with, organizational objectives. It is not concerned with managing the components. The goal of portfolio management is to ensure that the organization is "doing the right work," rather than "doing work right."

Table 1-1. Comparative Overview of Project, Program, and Portfolio Management

	PROJECTS	PROGRAMS	PORTFOLIOS
Scope	Projects have defined objectives. Scope is progressively elaborated throughout the project life cycle.	Programs have a larger scope and provide more significant benefits.	Portfolios have a business scope that changes with the strategic goals of the organization.
Change	Project managers expect change and implement processes to keep change managed and controlled.	The program manager must expect change from both inside and outside the program and be prepared to manage it.	Portfolio managers continually monitor changes in the broad environment.
Planning	Project managers progressively elaborate high-level information into detailed plans throughout the project life cycle.	Program managers develop the overall program plan and create high-level plans to guide detailed planning at the component level.	Portfolio managers create and maintain necessary processes and communication relative to the aggregate portfolio.
Management	Project managers manage the project team to meet the project objectives.	Program managers manage the program staff and the project managers; they provide vision and overall leadership.	Portfolio managers may manage or coordinate portfolio management staff.
Success	Success is measured by product and project quality, timeliness, budget compliance, and degree of customer satisfaction.	Success is measured by the degree to which the program satisfies the needs and benefits for which it was undertaken.	Success is measured in terms of aggregate performance of portfolio components.
Monitoring	Project managers monitor and control the work of producing the products, services or results that the project was undertaken to produce.	Program managers monitor the progress of program components to ensure the overall goals, schedules, budget, and benefits of the program will be met.	Portfolio managers monitor aggregate performance and value indicators.

1.4 The Link Between Portfolio Management and Organizational Governance

Organizations have governance frameworks in place to guide the execution of organizational activities. Organizational governance establishes the limits of power, rules of conduct, and protocols that organizations use to manage progress towards the achievement of their strategic goals. This is accomplished through controls intended to maximize the delivery of value while minimizing risk. For the purposes of this standard, organizational governance is the process by which an organization directs and controls its operations and strategic activities, and by which the organization responds to the legitimate rights, expectations, and desires of its stakeholders. Project Portfolio Governance is a set of interrelated organizational processes by which an organization prioritizes, selects, and allocates limited internal resources to best accomplish organizational objectives.

Portfolio management is one discipline within organizational governance. Organizations that do not link portfolio management to governance increase the risk that misaligned or low priority initiatives will consume critical resources. Therefore, applying the techniques of portfolio management within the context of organizational governance provides reasonable assurance that the organizational strategy can be achieved.

Portfolio management is both a framework and a management activity. The framework provides the means to translate the organizational strategy into a portfolio of strategic and operational initiatives. The management activity ensures actualization of those initiatives through the use of organizational resources.

Figure 1-2 illustrates the relationships between organizational governance, operational management, and management of initiatives that comprise the portfolio. Governance principles ensure alignment between the resulting activities and the organizational strategy.

In this figure, the controls that comprise organizational governance cascade to the domains of portfolio, program, and project management. As the portfolio is managed, these controls are applied to maximize the likelihood of the success of the organization's strategy. Managing these controls against the portfolio is the responsibility of the portfolio manager, whose role is detailed in Section 1.8. The processes that guide execution of Portfolio Governance are discussed in Chapter 4.

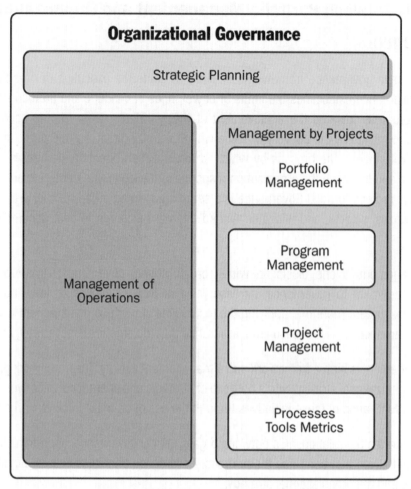

Figure 1-2. Relationships among Organizational Governance, Operations, and Portfolio Management

1.5 The Relationship between Portfolio Management and Organizational Strategy

Organizations build strategy to define how their vision will be achieved. The vision is enabled by the mission, which directs the execution of the strategy. For the purposes of this standard, organizational strategy is a plan that describes how the company's strengths and core competencies will be used to:

- Capitalize on opportunities,
- Minimize the impact of threats,
- Respond to changes in the market, and
- Reinforce focus on critical operational activities.

This standard presumes that the organization has a strategic plan accompanied by mission and vision statements as well as strategic goals and objectives. The goal of linking portfolio management to the strategy is to balance the use of resources to maximize value in executing strategic and operational activities.

The organizational strategy is a result of the strategic planning cycle, where the vision and mission are translated into a strategic plan. The strategic plan is subdivided into a set of initiatives that are influenced by market dynamics, customer and partner requests, shareholders, government regulations, and competitor plans and actions. These initiatives establish strategic and operational portfolios to be executed in the planned period.

Figure 1-3 depicts a general relationship between the strategic and operational processes in an organization.

Figure 1-3. The Organizational Context of Portfolio Management

"Vision," "mission," and "organizational strategy and objectives" illustrate the components used to *set* the organization's performance targets. "High-level operations planning and management" and "project portfolio planning and management" *establish* the distinct initiatives required to achieve the organization's performance targets. "Management of on-going operations" and "management of authorized programs and projects" correspond to *executing* the operational, program, and project activities to realize the organization's performance targets.

The shaded section, "project portfolio planning and management," depicts the relationship between organizational strategy, strategic planning, and management activities. This relationship is highlighted due to the traditional focus of portfolio management on strategic project planning. To guide the "management of authorized programs and projects," a project portfolio is created. This portfolio, which links the organizational

---

strategy to a set of prioritized programs and projects, addresses the relevant internal and external business drivers referenced as objectives in the strategic plan.

The ultimate goal of linking portfolio management with organizational strategy is to establish a balanced, executable plan that will help the organization achieve its goals. The impact of the portfolio plan upon strategy is attained by the five areas shown below:

1. **Maintaining portfolio alignment.** Each component should be aligned to one or more strategic goals. Alignment cannot occur without a clear understanding of those goals, and any proposal would describe how it supports the goals.

2. **Allocating financial resources.** The priority of each component guides financial allocation decisions, while at the same time each component requires an allocation if it is to be executed.

3. **Allocating human resources.** The priority of each component guides resource planning, hiring efforts, and time and skill allocations.

4. **Measuring component contributions.** If the purpose of undertaking the component is to achieve a strategic goal, its contribution must be measured in the context of that goal.

5. **Strategic risk management.** Each component should be evaluated for risks and how those risks may impact the achievement of the strategic goals.

1.6 The Relationships Among Portfolio, Program, and Project Management

A portfolio has a parent-child relationship with its components, just as a program has a parent-child relationship with its projects. The components are managed according to frameworks, such as *A Guide to the Project Management Body of Knowledge (PMBOK® Guide) – Fourth Edition* and *The Standard for Program Management* – Second Edition, and are periodically measured to gauge the likelihood of the components achieving their goals. An organization evaluates the portfolio components using the tools and techniques within the portfolio management processes. These processes, such as the Selection and Portfolio Balancing processes, are detailed later in this standard.

When considering Portfolio Governance, the roles of executive, portfolio, program, project, and operations management are all interrelated. These relationships are shown in Figure 1-4. In smaller organizations, the roles of the executive and portfolio management may be combined into one. This standard presumes that the organization has the project management processes to support and implement portfolio management.

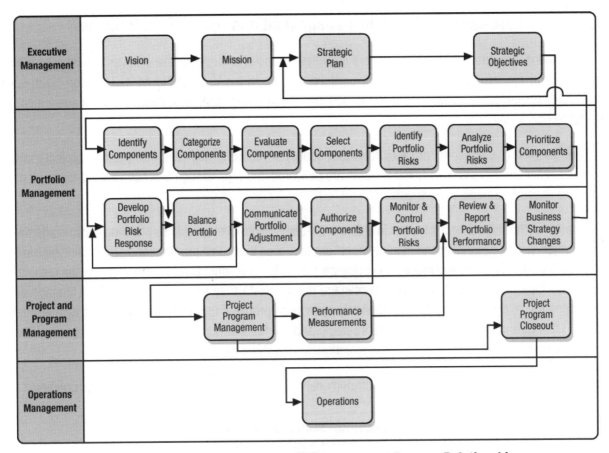

Figure 1-4. Cross-Company Portfolio Management Process Relationships

1.7 The Link Between Portfolio Management and Operations Management

Portfolio management interacts with and impacts a number of organizational functions. Functional groups can be stakeholders in the portfolio and can also serve as sponsors of various components. The achievement of portfolio objectives may impact functional groups within an organization in their daily operations. Moreover, an operational budget may be influenced by portfolio management decisions, including allocation of resources to support portfolio components.

"Operations" is a term used to describe day-to-day organizational activities. The organization's operations may include production, manufacturing, finance, marketing, legal, information services, human resources, and administrative services to name just a few.

Processes and deliverables used by operational management are often outputs of the portfolio components. Therefore, the portfolio management team must manage relationships and interfaces with operations effectively if the full value of each component is to be realized.

1.7.1 The Link Between Portfolio Management and Operational Projects

Operational projects (groups of operational activities managed as projects) are often as critical as strategic projects, and are translated into a distinct portfolio defined in the area of Figure 1-3 labeled "high-level operations planning and management." This portfolio encompasses the work executed in "management of on-going operations."

The portfolio of operational projects links that subset of recurring activities managed as projects to the organizational strategy. As operational projects are delivered, the organization will have a solid foundation on which to execute strategic components.

Therefore, the outputs from the areas in Figure 1-3 labeled "high-level operations planning and management" and "project portfolio planning and management" are portfolios that guide program and project activities in the planned period. This idea is expanded upon in Figure 1-5. As the components move into initiation, the respective areas use their management processes to manage deliveries. As they are executed, portfolio management maintains the relationships among components to monitor progress and maintain alignment with strategic goals. Therefore, at the highest level, the strategic and operational portfolios are ultimately managed as a single, comprehensive portfolio of work being undertaken by the organization.

Figure 1-5 details the logical flow from strategy definition to comprehensive project portfolio creation.

Figure 1-5. Building a Comprehensive Project Portfolio

1.7.2 Operational Stakeholders in Portfolio Management

The portfolio management process must also engage key stakeholders from operations to ensure alignment between the portfolio components and potential impacts to these operations. The following examples illustrate the relationship between operations and portfolio management:

.1 Finance

Effective management of the portfolio requires tangible, timely, and accurate financial information. The portfolio manager considers financial goals and objectives in the management of a portfolio. Therefore, the finance function may monitor portfolio budgets, compare project spending with the allocated budget, and examine benefits realized. This ensures that financial plan adjustments are made and projected savings are quantifiable and delivered.

.2 Marketing

Market analysis, benchmarking, and research play a significant role in portfolio management as the portfolio components are driven by such considerations as market opportunity or competitive advantage. For a nonprofit, government, or military organization, a similar analysis of value-for-money or value-to-organizational-mission is needed for component selection and management.

.3 Human Resources

By looking at the portfolio of components, the human resources function can identify the skills and qualifications needed for success and then work to ensure skilled resources are available when needed. The human resources function also works to facilitate resource realignment and mitigate the negative impact on people resulting from organizational changes that result when portfolio components are delivered.

.4 Information Technology

Portfolio management usually has a significant impact on information technology operations. Portfolio components often require support from information technology operations, including business process analysis, development, service, help desk support, infrastructure support, and on-going application maintenance. For example, a manufacturing portfolio could contain a program to install an Enterprise Resource Planning (ERP) system for the organization. This portfolio could potentially increase help desk support, network traffic, and support obligations for an application development team. The portfolio manager must take into account these impacts to ensure that infrastructure and properly trained resources are adequate to support the portfolio's components.

1.8 Role of the Portfolio Manager

The portfolio manager, typically a senior manager or a member of the senior management team, is responsible for establishing, monitoring, and managing assigned portfolios in the following ways:

- Establishing and/or maintaining a framework (a conceptual structure of ideas) and methodology (a body of methods and rules) for portfolio management within the organization;

- Establishing and/or maintaining relevant portfolio management processes (e.g., risk management);

- Guiding the selection, prioritization, and balancing of the portfolio to ensure the components align with strategic goals and organizational priorities;

- Establishing and maintaining appropriate infrastructure and systems to support portfolio management processes;

- Continuously reviewing, reallocating, reprioritizing, and optimizing the portfolio, and ensuring ongoing compliance with evolving organizational goals and market opportunities;

- Providing key stakeholders with timely assessment of component selection, prioritization and performance, as well as early identification of (and intervention into) portfolio-level issues and risks that are impacting performance;

- Measuring and monitoring the value to the organization through key performance indicators, such as return on investment (ROI), net present value (NPV), payback period (PP), meeting legal and regulatory requirements, and achieving the educational needs of current or future stakeholders, etc.;

- Supporting senior level decision making by ensuring timely and consistent communication to stakeholders on progress, changes, and impact on portfolio components;

- Participating in program and project reviews to reflect senior level support, leadership, and involvement in important matters; and

- Adhering to ethical standards so as to maintain the integrity of the discipline.

In order to succeed in this role, the portfolio manager should apply expertise in all of the following areas with the support of a program/project management office, as needed:

1.8.1 Strategic Alignment

A portfolio manager must understand the organization's strategic goals and priorities, and how the portfolio supports them. Both financial and non-financial benefits and risks to the organization must be taken into account. The portfolio manager typically does not create the organization's strategy, but may participate in the process, depending on the specific organization. However, the portfolio manager does play a key role in implementing the strategy by monitoring execution of initiatives in support of it and by communicating results.

1.8.2 Portfolio Management Methods and Techniques

The portfolio manager must have expertise in the use of portfolio management methods and techniques that include both qualitative and quantitative measures. Some examples are:

- Project selection methods;

- Decision support tools and models, such as financial targets (return on investment (ROI), internal rate of return (IRR), etc.), simulation techniques, and constraint management;

- Prioritization algorithms;

- Capability and capacity modeling methods and tools;

- Project and program auditing techniques; and

- Organizational and Portfolio Risk Management.

1.8.3 Program and Project Management Methods and Techniques

The portfolio manager must have expertise in project and program management to evaluate how components and the portfolio overall are progressing. Further, the portfolio manager must understand both high-level project reporting and the details needed to determine whether each component's management is satisfactory. Life-cycle oversight methods, such as monitoring compliance with standards, evaluating progress through earned value analysis, etc., should be aligned with the organization's project and program management processes.

1.8.4 Process Development and Continuous Improvement

The portfolio manager must be knowledgeable in process development and continuous improvement. This will help develop the most suitable portfolio management processes. In addition to process modeling techniques, the portfolio manager should be knowledgeable in quality principles and methodologies, such as Total Quality Management (TQM), Continuous Quality Improvement (CQI), Lean, and Six Sigma.

1.8.5 General Business Skills

Typically, an effective portfolio manager has well-developed business acumen. The portfolio manager has knowledge of relevant markets, the customer base, competition, trends, standards, legal and regulatory environments, and appropriate code of conduct.

A portfolio manager should also have analytical skills to monitor the portfolio based on portfolio performance reports and measures. These competencies include:

- Understanding of key financial principles;

- Ability to create, use, and apply appropriate key performance indicators (KPIs) in portfolio performance measurement;

- Ability to analyze financial information and perform trend analysis; and

- Ability to effectively evaluate business cases in the portfolio selection process.

1.8.6 General Management Skills

An effective portfolio manager has well-developed leadership and management skills and is able to interact effectively with executives, management, and other stakeholders. Further, a portfolio manager is adept in managing people through recruitment and retention, goal-setting, performance evaluation, reward and recognition, succession planning, and employee development. Employee development may include mentoring, coaching, motivating, and training of personnel.

General management skills should be exercised in alignment with the organization's culture, maturity, and policies, and with respect to cultural and other differences between individuals. Further, the portfolio manager usually possesses and exercises well-developed skills in communication, team building, planning, conflict resolution, contract negotiation, meeting facilitation, decision making, and removing organizational barriers to success. The portfolio manager must be able to adapt to divergent organizational decision-making models, ranging from autocratic to collegial, often in the same organization.

1.8.7 Stakeholder Management

An effective portfolio manager is adept at working with portfolio stakeholders in order to maximize portfolio and organizational performance. A portfolio manager should communicate frequently with stakeholders using modes and techniques appropriate for the context. The portfolio manager must deal effectively with executives, managers, project and program managers, and other internal and external stakeholders in ways appropriate to the individuals and their roles.

1.8.8 Risk and Opportunity Management

An effective portfolio manager understands how to manage risks and opportunities at the composite level, giving consideration to all portfolio dynamics, such as fiscal constraints, window of opportunity, component constraints, and stakeholder dynamics. Risk and opportunity management is a structured process for assessing and analyzing portfolio risks and opportunities with the goal of capitalizing on the potential opportunities and mitigating those events, activities, or circumstances that can adversely impact the project. Risk management is critical where interdependencies exist between high-priority components, where the cost of component failure is significant, or when risks of one component raise the risks in another component. Opportunity management identifies and exploits the potential improvements in component performance that may increase quality, customer satisfaction, service levels, and productivity for both components and the organization. Opportunity management may generate new components as well.

1.9 Portfolio Management Reporting and Metrics

Reporting in the portfolio management context refers to understanding portfolio content and measuring component performance. Such reporting is tightly linked with other types of organizational reporting to drive decisions regarding priority, balancing, and direction of the portfolio. Portfolio reporting also facilitates effective communication between the portfolio sponsor and portfolio stakeholders (e.g., program managers, project managers, portfolio manager, and operations management).

Portfolio reporting should focus on satisfying the information needs of the portfolio sponsors and provide them with metrics that they can use to ensure the portfolios are meeting the sponsors' and the organization's objectives. It should enable the portfolio sponsors to quickly understand the status of their portfolios' financial position, risks, and issues. Portfolio reporting should also enable sponsors to understand if their portfolios are achieving the benefits they were intended to realize.

To a lesser degree, portfolio reporting should also provide individuals responsible for executing portfolio components with meaningful information on the status of their respective components in the context of other portfolio components. This level of portfolio reporting is important to optimize resource utilization.

1.9.1 Portfolio Reporting and the PMO

Many organizations place responsibility for reporting the effectiveness of portfolio components with a project management office (PMO). The PMO can provide information on the total investment in a component to serve as an input for monitoring the component's value. Some organizations rely on a dashboard to present information at a glance. Examples of potential dashboard views are:

- **Organization Portfolio Overall Health**—Reporting the overall status of the portfolio. This provides the portfolio sponsor with a quick view on how the entire portfolio is performing against predefined key performance indicators (KPIs).

- **Organization Strategic Goal Achievement**—Reporting the extent to which components will or have contributed to organization strategic goals. This is a key area of reporting that is often overlooked. If a portfolio is not directly supporting an organization's goals, the portfolio sponsor should question the value of investing in the portfolio.

- **Organization Risk Profile**—Reporting the composite risk level of the portfolio and the impact of a component's risk on the portfolio's overall risk. The portfolio sponsor should be able to determine through reporting that the risks accepted by the organization are appropriate for the benefits that will be achieved by the portfolio. Assessing risk is critical to determining whether or not to include a component in the portfolio. Managing risk is a key criterion for portfolio component success.

- **Organization Resource Capability**—Reporting the resource usage of the organization and individual components in the portfolio, including planned vs. actual. Portfolio stakeholders should ensure that the right resources are focused on the right projects at the right time. The reports help optimize resources within and across portfolios to achieve the organization's strategic objectives.

- **Organization Financial Information**—Reporting financial data (data used to measure progress and maintain control) and the value received from the component are both important for selecting components to include and maintain within the portfolio.

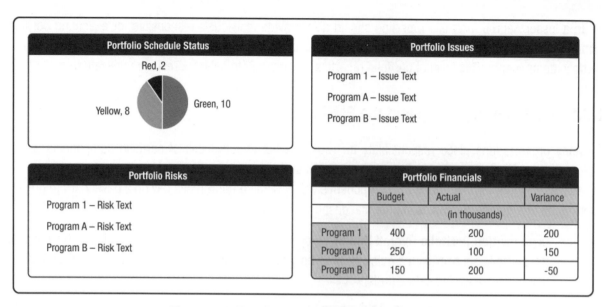

Figure 1-6. Example of a Portfolio Dashboard

1.9.2 Portfolio Management Metrics

The portfolio manager should base portfolio reporting on a predefined, preapproved set of metrics that monitor strategic goal achievement, financial contribution, stakeholder satisfaction, risk profile, and resource utilization. Metrics measure quantitative or qualitative information aggregated from the portfolio components.

The selected metrics should be relevant to the organization's goals and aligned with its other performance metrics. The portfolio manager should be prepared to develop new metrics when appropriate and remove metrics that are no longer relevant to the stakeholders or that no longer support the organization's goals. The quantity of metrics should not overwhelm the stakeholders to ensure the metrics are actively tracked and understood. Some examples of portfolio metrics are:

- Quantitative measures:
  - ○ Increase in revenue attributable to the portfolio,
  - ○ Development of new markets and expansion of customer base as a result of the portfolio,
  - ○ Cost reductions attributable to the portfolio,
  - ○ Change in net present value (NPV) of the portfolio,
  - ○ Return on investment (ROI) from the portfolio,
  - ○ Internal rate of return (IRR) of the portfolio,
  - ○ Degree to which portfolio and business risks have been reduced by undertaking the portfolio components,
  - ○ Availability of resources needed to support the portfolio components, both as planned and in execution,

- o Percentage by which cycle times are reduced due to the portfolio, and

- o Change in quality improvement scores attributable to the portfolio.

- Qualitative benefits:

- o Degree of strategic alignment, and

- o Recognition of legal and regulatory compliance.

There are similarities among project, program, and portfolio management, particularly in the need to measure whether the expected value is realized. Portfolio metrics, however, must meet the decision-making needs of portfolio stakeholders, and so focus more on progress toward the organization's financial, customer satisfaction, efficiency, risk, and diversification goals. As a result, portfolio metrics are less concerned with specific lifecycles and more focused on monitoring progress toward achieving an organization's goals. By contrast, project and program management metrics illustrate the health at a given point in time and progress toward producing deliverables. Project metrics focus on the individual project and are tracked over time so trends can be identified, analyzed, and addressed. While similar metrics may apply to a program, program metrics tend to consolidate and summarize performance of the various constituent projects. In both cases, maintaining control over the life cycle is more significant than it is with portfolio metrics.

CHAPTER 2

PORTFOLIO MANAGEMENT OVERVIEW AND ORGANIZATION

Portfolio management is a process that enables executive management to meet organization goals and objectives through efficient decision making concerning projects and other work, either directly or under programs. Portfolio management is performed in an environment broader than the portfolio itself: its roles and processes span the organization. This chapter describes the key components of the portfolio management context in the following sections:

2.1 Portfolio Management Process Overview

2.2 Portfolio Stakeholder Roles and Responsibilities

2.3 Organizational Influences

2.1 Portfolio Management Process Overview

2.1.1 Strategy and Investment Alignment

Portfolio management includes processes to identify, categorize, evaluate, select, prioritize, balance, and authorize components within the portfolio. The portfolio managers may evaluate the portfolio components and the portfolio as a whole as to how well they are performing in relation to the key indicators and the strategic plan. During a typical business cycle, the portfolio manager will monitor and validate components relative to the following:

- Alignment with corporate strategy,

- Viability as part of the portfolio, based on key performance indicators and an acceptable level of risk,

- Value and relationship to other portfolio components,

- Available resources and portfolio priorities, and

- Additions and deletions of portfolio components.

The executive level, through the definition and articulation of the strategic goals and objectives, determines the organization's overall strategy. The organization strategy and corresponding business goals are inputs to the portfolio management process. They drive the portfolio management process to ensure that components are aligned to achieve the organization's goals. Based on these inputs, the portfolio management team will holistically select, prioritize, and approve proposed portfolio components. Through review of strategic and tactical capabilities and gaps, the portfolio management process provides feedback useful for the planning and

---

management of resource demand and for monitoring the health of the portfolio. The portfolio manager must report portfolio performance as it relates to achieving the organization's planned strategy.

The portfolio management team must also review the portfolio for balance (short-term versus long-term return and risk versus benefit) and negotiate agreement(s) with relevant strategic stakeholders (e.g. executive management, operations, and/or program management).

An important strategic input to the portfolio management process concerns resource management. The balance of a portfolio must be achievable within strategic resource levels. The selection of components and their prioritization must be consistent with the overall resource availability acknowledging that various resources may be constrained. Examples are current expense or capital, internal employee skills, or technical equipment.

Once a portfolio component is authorized, the program/project manager assumes control of the component and applies the correct management processes to ensure that the work is done effectively and efficiently. The responsible program/project managers will monitor planned to actual performance (schedule, budget, resources, quality, and scope) and will provide feedback to the portfolio management team. The portfolio management team should establish criteria for governance actions, such as deciding when projects/programs should proceed, be terminated, or suspended prior to originally planned completion dates. The processes for project and program management are described in these PMI standards: *The Standard for Program Management* – Second Edition and *A Guide to the Project Management Body of Knowledge* (PMBOK® Guide) – Fourth Edition, respectively.

The portfolio management process also requires integration with the strategic planning process regarding current and future state analysis. This drives strategic changes to ensure that the planned (active and future) components continue to support the strategic goals. For example, if strategic planning determines that a goal is no longer valid for the organization, the portfolio management team should review the portfolio and recommend the reassessment of any components that are in place to achieve a now obsolete goal.

Organizations normally apply some form of control over portfolio components. For example, a phase gate review is commonly applied to projects in those portfolios concentrating on research activities. Governance processes are often characterized by regular reviews (review meetings) at key decision milestones during the life of the project. Senior stakeholders in governance roles analyze the risk and reward associated with continuing the project. The purpose is to assess the probability of success of all aspects of the project as it progresses. This means that every aspect of the project is assessed at each review meeting. For instance, the legal, engineering, financial, and commercial aspects of the product are included in the early-stage assessments when the immediate investment decision is about research and development. As the project progresses, the legal, engineering, scientific, and other aspects continue to be assessed. The significance for the portfolio manager is that the assessment results become part of the portfolio information.

2.1.2   Portfolio Component Management Life Cycle

As described previously, each component passes through a number of steps prior to being authorized and then implemented. Table 2-1 provides an overview of the possible values of component status.

In order to provide effective control of the management of the portfolio, two main reviews are carried out: the first, near the beginning of the *Alignment Process Group*, once component selection has been completed; the second completes the *Alignment Process Group processes* once a balanced portfolio has been assembled; the *Monitoring and Controlling Process Group processes* can then commence.

Table 2-1. Component Processing Leading to Authorization

PROCESS	RESULTANT STATE	COMMENT
Identify Components	• Identified	
Categorize Components	• Categorized	
Evaluate Components	• Evaluated • Recommended	• All categorized components are evaluated: only some are recommended
Select Components	• Selected • Rejected • Pending	• Selected means that the component is on a short list, not that it will immediately go into the portfolio • Pending is similar to inactivated, except it has never attained the priority level even to be authorized; the component remains in the list of candidate components for the next prioritization
Prioritize Components	• Prioritized • Reprioritized	• The priority of a component can be revised
Balance Components	• Approved • Rejected • Inactivated • Terminated	• Rejection can occur at this stage or earlier, during selection
Authorize Components	• Authorized	

2.1.3   Portfolio Management Process Cycle

Organizations have many regular business processes. External requirements (such as fiscal reporting) or internal requirements (such as quarterly budget revisions) may drive these business processes. While portfolio management is a continuous business process, certain activities are invoked during a given year as appropriate to the organization. The purpose is to represent portfolio activities in those other business processes. For example, selection and authorization of components can be part of annual planning or strategic review with quarterly or semi-annual updates. Performance monitoring of the portfolio is usually continuous. Revising the portfolio mix may be required when disruptions to the organization occur. Once established, the portfolio management process does not end—except when the organization chooses to abandon the portfolio management approach or the organization ceases to exist.

2.1.4   Establishing a Portfolio Management Process

As stated in this chapter, portfolio management is a process with regular, repeating activities for the management of decisions related to portfolio components and the integration with other processes. This standard describes the process and the context in which it functions.

To establish a new portfolio management process where none exists or a new one is needed as a result of a merger or acquisition, there must be an initiative to define the process. The objective of a "defining" step is to establish the following:

- Organizational structure and performance measurement system that defines the boundaries, authorities, responsibilities, and tasks;
- Exercise of authority and control for the investment portfolio; and
- Project portfolio management process auditing function and audit process.

The following are examples of documents developed during the "defining" step:

- Project portfolio management organizational structure,
- Project portfolio management roles and responsibilities,
- Project portfolio management plan,
- Project portfolio management risk management plan,
- Project portfolio management communications plan,
- Project portfolio management component authorization process, and
- Project portfolio management process "governance" process/plan.

The product or outcome of the "defining" step is a functioning portfolio management process as described in this standard.

2.2 Portfolio Stakeholder Roles and Responsibilities

Portfolio stakeholders are individuals or groups whose interests may be positively or negatively affected by portfolio components or portfolio management processes. They may also exert influence over the portfolio, its components, processes, and decisions. The level of involvement by stakeholders may vary from organization to organization or from portfolio to portfolio within an organization.

Depending upon the specific project supervision approach (such as a phase-gate), certain stakeholders may be specifically identified according to the goals and risk management strategies for the portfolio.

The roles and responsibilities of stakeholders are described in the following sections.

2.2.1 Executive Review Board

Executive management evaluates, selects, prioritizes, and controls project activity. The cross-functional and integrated executive review board determines and authorizes the scope of control of the portfolio management board(s) to direct portfolio management operational activity. Input to the project alignment decision-making process includes, but is not limited to, the business vision, implementation strategy, resource capacity, and short- and long-term business plans. In smaller organizations, executive management may assume all or some of the portfolio management responsibilities including making review board decisions.

2.2.2 Portfolio Process Group

The role of the portfolio Process Group is focused on administration. Its mission is to design, validate, and implement the framework, and to document best practices and supporting workflow processes to govern and enable portfolio management within the organization. One specific deliverable could be a portfolio dashboard template for showing the performance of a portfolio relative to the business goals.

2.2.3 Portfolio Management Board

The portfolio management board's role is to make decisions about investments and priorities for the components of the portfolio and to ensure the project portfolio management process is followed. The board is made up of those individuals with the requisite authority, knowledge, and experience to ensure the alignment of strategy and organizational goals with portfolio components. The board has the authority to evaluate the portfolio performance and to make resourcing, investment, and priority decisions as needed. Recommendations may include new portfolio components, the suspension or change of existing components, and the reallocation of scarce resources between components.

2.2.4 Portfolio Managers

Portfolio managers or portfolio management teams are responsible for the execution of the portfolio management process for a particular portfolio. Portfolio managers receive performance information on component performance and progress, and they convey to the portfolio management board how the components as a whole are aligned with the strategic goals and provide appropriate recommendations or options for action. They also ensure that timetables for portfolio management processes are maintained and followed and that the managers of portfolio components (projects, programs, and other work) receive and provide the information required under the portfolio management processes. They are the primary conduit between managers of portfolio components and the portfolio management board.

2.2.5 Sponsors

Sponsors champion approval of their components (projects, programs, and other work). To ensure approval, a sponsor must aid in supplying a viable business case to the portfolio management board or other oversight team. Once the component is approved, the sponsor must help ensure that it performs according to plan and achieves its strategic goals.

2.2.6   Program Managers

The program manager is responsible for ensuring that the overall program structure and program management processes enable the component teams to successfully complete their work and that the components' deliverables can be integrated into the program's end product, service, results and/or benefits. Program managers also ensure projects are organized and executed in a consistent manner and/or fulfilled within established standards. The PMO supports the program manager by providing the information needed to make decisions that guide the program and by providing administrative support in managing schedules, budgets, risks, and the other areas required for effective program management.

2.2.7   Project Managers

Project managers are responsible for the effective planning, execution, monitoring, and delivery of the assigned projects in accordance with corresponding objectives and specifications. Project managers provide project performance indicators, directly or indirectly, to the portfolio management board. This information will be used with other criteria to determine which projects will be continued.

The project manager may also supply a recovery plan for projects in jeopardy and be responsible for the budget and schedule of all assigned projects. Additionally, the project manager's peer group of other project managers is a stakeholder group in the portfolio management process. Both the project manager and portfolio management will benefit from formal or informal networks of project managers in the organization. These networks can help to facilitate a balanced distribution of scarce resources through improved communication and sharing of best practices.

2.2.8   Program/Project Management Office

The program or project management office (PMO) coordinates management of those components in its domain. The domain may be a specific area of the organization or class of projects or programs. The responsibilities of a PMO can include the following: providing project management support functions, managing day-to-day operations of the system or systems that support portfolio management, resourcing and directly managing a component or category of components. The role and activities of a PMO are addressed in the relevant PMI standards: *A Guide to the Project Management Body of Knowledge (PMBOK® Guide)* – Fourth Edition and *The Standard for Program Management* – Second Edition.

The establishment of a PMO can help to transform the culture of the organization. For example, the existence of a PMO can highlight the need for a structured and formal governance process and body where none has existed before. This, in turn, generates further benefits, discipline, and understanding for the organization. The newly established executive review board would then set the expectations for the derived benefits of portfolio management as they authorize the implementation of portfolio management processes.

2.2.9　Project Team

A project team executes planned activities on its particular project to ensure the project continues to successful completion. They also provide project performance and status metrics as input to the portfolio management process.

2.2.10　Marketing Management

Marketing performs analysis, benchmarking, and research to determine position relative to the market and the competition. Portfolio component decisions may be driven by such considerations as pricing, product growth, market opportunity, or competitive advantage. For a non-profit, governmental, or military organization, a similar analysis of value-for-money or value-to-organizational-mission is needed for component selection and management.

2.2.11　Operations Management

Operations management is responsible for the ongoing business operations including manufacturing, distribution, and customer service centers. It is normally in operational management where benefit realization is monitored and measured.

2.2.12　Engineering Management

Engineering management is responsible for establishing the facilities by which ongoing delivery of the product is provided. During the life of the project, the ability to create the production infrastructure is assured by the engineering function.

2.2.13　Legal Management

Legal management is responsible for ensuring that the demands of the regulatory environment are satisfied during the execution of projects within the portfolio and that the final products are legally acceptable. The stringency of legal requirements varies widely from industry to industry and country to country.

2.2.14　Human Resources Management

Human resources management is responsible for maintaining the correct balance of staff and competencies based on the drivers of the strategic plan and marketplace pressures. The organization's structure (e.g., projectized, centralized, or decentralized) is often determined based on the critical success factors of the strategic business plan.

2.2.15 Functional Managers

Functional managers ensure that proper resources are allocated to the portfolio components and that those resources are performing in accordance with plans. They may also be responsible for the operation of processes or other ongoing business activities. In this case, they are also responsible for the resources that support these operations and may have to ensure sufficient resources are available for both programs/projects and operations.

Functional managers are also responsible for ensuring that skills and capabilities are kept current and aligned to the long term as well as the immediate needs of the organization. Functional managers may provide technical backup and coaching as appropriate to their staff.

2.2.16 Finance Managers

Finance managers perform financial analyses on components, review portfolio budget performance, and make recommendations to the appropriate oversight entity. They also provide management information needed by program and project managers to assess variances and develop status reports.

2.2.17 Customers

Customers, both internal and external, benefit from successful implementation and delivery of portfolio components. Customer satisfaction may be one of the strategic drivers that determines the mix and priority of the components within the portfolio.

2.2.18 Vendors/Business Partners

Business partners and vendors are also key stakeholders in managing the project portfolio. Most organizations involve their business partners and/or vendors in executing various programs/projects. It is very important to involve them, to the extent needed, in the overall portfolio management process.

2.3 Organizational Influences

Successful portfolio management means that all management levels must effectively support the effort and communicate clearly and consistently the value of portfolio management to the organization.

When making allocation decisions, organizations are influenced by a variety of constraints and dynamics brought to bear by the stakeholders. The art of portfolio management is to balance stakeholder interests, both short-term and long-term, while staying aligned with the business' strategic goals. The portfolio manager needs to make decisions in the best interest of the overall portfolio performance regardless of the impact to individual components. The forces influencing portfolio management are identified in the following sections.

2.3.1 Organizational Culture

The organization as a whole must understand the business need for portfolio management and commit its leadership, people, processes, and tools to make it successful. It is important that the philosophy of portfolio management permeates the entire organization. This means that all other activities and processes take into account the impact on or influence of portfolio management, even if the effect is slight. For instance, general performance measures should be compatible and complementary with those used for assessing portfolio components.

The term organizational maturity can be applied to the acceptance of portfolio management in the same way as it can to project management. The level of application and the success of portfolio management are directly affected by the level of maturity in the organization. Lack of organizational support for the concept and approach of portfolio management would be a major obstacle to portfolio management success. The portfolio management process and the decisions resulting from it must be accepted at all levels within the organization. There is a danger that while the process is accepted conceptually by senior executives in the organization, the resulting decisions may not be. This failure to accept and act on portfolio management decisions may pervade the organization.

Another important element is the organization's ability to accept and implement the changes recommended by the portfolio management processes. This is a different issue from that described previously about accepting decisions resulting from the portfolio management process. Not recognizing and formalizing the organization's ability to handle change can also be a major obstacle to fully realizing the improvement expected from the portfolio. Each component of the portfolio should consistently apply similar techniques to facilitate and handle organizational change. The degree of organizational change the organization is willing to accept as a whole may be one of the factors used in determining the balance of the portfolio. This is related to the strategic goals of the organization which serve as inputs to the portfolio decision process. Strategic goals will precipitate some expected level of change to the organization's people, processes, products, and technologies.

2.3.2 Economic Impact

Financial conditions may place a premium on, or an increased opportunity for, portfolio management to assist in decision making with regard to projects that are failing or proceeding well. Project success may be expressed in terms of negative or positive cash flow, time to market, and resource balancing. The intent is to ensure that a higher percentage of projects will be successful.

2.3.3 Organizational Impacts

This topic is related to that of organizational culture described in Section 2.3.1. The distinction is that organizational impact refers to the impact that portfolio management has on the organization rather than on the cultural environment in which portfolio management operates.

Effective portfolio management can have positive impacts across the organization by facilitating local planning in alignment with strategic goals. Conversely, a lack of efficient and effective processes and procedures in other functional areas of the organization can have a considerable impact on portfolio management. An example is the lack of a consistent resource assignment process in support of the execution of projects and programs approved through portfolio management decisions. Those involved in the portfolio management process will need to factor this into corresponding plans and decisions.

2.3.4   Enterprise Environmental Factors

Enterprise environmental factors (EEFs) refer to any or all external environmental factors and internal organizational environmental factors described in Sections 2.3.1 and 2.3.3 that surround or influence a portfolio's success. They are characterized by being decided externally to the organization outside of its direct control, yet they impact the portfolio management decision processes.

Enterprise environmental factors may constrain portfolio management options and may have a positive or negative influence on the outcome. Enterprise environmental factors include, but are not limited to:

- Organizational culture and structure described in Sections 2.3.1 and 2.3.3;

- Legal constraints;

- Governmental or industry standards (e.g., regulatory agency regulations, codes of conduct, product standards, quality standards, and workmanship standards);

- Infrastructure (e.g., existing facilities and capital equipment);

- Existing human resources (e.g., skills, disciplines, and knowledge, such as design, development, law, contracting, and purchasing);

- Personnel administration (e.g., hiring and firing guidelines, employee performance reviews, and training records);

- Company work authorization systems;

- Marketplace conditions;

- Stakeholder risk tolerances;

- Commercial databases (e.g., standardized cost estimating data, industry risk study information, and risk databases); and

- Project management information systems (e.g., an automated tool suite, such as a scheduling software tool, a configuration management system, an information collection and distribution system, or web interfaces to other online automated systems).

SECTION II

THE STANDARD FOR PORTFOLIO MANAGEMENT

Chapter 3

- Portfolio Management Processes

CHAPTER 3

PORTFOLIO MANAGEMENT PROCESSES

Portfolio management is a set of inter-related business management processes that facilitate informed decision making and objective investment decisions. The portfolio components and management processes are selected to produce specific benefits (aggregate performance) to the organization; therefore, selecting portfolio management processes is a strategic decision.

In order to be successful, the portfolio management team must:

- Understand the organization's strategic plan,
- Establish strategic organizational criteria for managing the portfolio,
- Consider all of the organization's projects, programs, and other portfolio components, and
- Follow agreed-upon processes mandated by the organization or selected by the team.

Portfolio management is accomplished through processes using relevant knowledge, skills, tools, and techniques that receive inputs and generate outputs. A process is a set of interrelated actions and activities performed to achieve a pre-specified product, result, or service. Each process is characterized by its inputs, the tools and techniques that can be applied, and the resulting outputs.

A portfolio manager must understand the impact of the selected portfolio management processes on the expected business results delivered by the portfolio. It will not be possible to realize an organization's vision, mission, and strategy through selected goals, objectives, priorities, and processes without accurately measuring the benefits to the business.

This standard covers the processes needed to make decisions about components and identifies those portfolio management processes that have been recognized as generally accepted good practices for project portfolios. These processes apply globally and across industry groups. Generally accepted practice means there is general agreement that the application of these portfolio management processes enhances the probability of success over time.

This does not mean that the processes described should always be applied uniformly for all portfolios. Each portfolio management team is always responsible for determining what process is appropriate for a given organization—and the appropriate degree of rigor for each process—and for any given portfolio.

Portfolio managers should address each process and its constituent inputs and outputs. They should use this chapter as a high-level guide for those processes that they must consider when managing a portfolio.

This standard presents and describes the key elements for portfolio management. This standard is not prescriptive in nature and therefore does not specify the means by which an organization should implement the portfolio management processes described herein. This standard presumes that the organization has a strategic plan accompanied by mission and vision statements as well as strategic goals and objectives. In order to implement the portfolio processes presented here, the reader must assume that the following conditions exist:

- Organization—including management—embraces the practice of portfolio management,

- Proposed projects and programs need to be evaluated,

- Appropriately skilled staff members are available to manage the portfolio,

- Project management processes exist,

- The organizational roles and responsibilities are defined, and

- Communication mechanisms exist to communicate business decisions throughout the organization.

The required portfolio management processes aggregate into two Portfolio Management Process Groups (see Figure 3-1). These groups have interdependencies and the portfolio management team performs these Process Groups in the management of each portfolio. Constituent processes can also interact, both within their particular Process Group and with the other Portfolio Management Process Group. The portfolio management team often repeats these group and individual constituent processes during the portfolio management process. The two Portfolio Management Process Groups are:

- **Aligning Process Group.** Determines how components will be categorized, evaluated, selected for inclusion, and managed in the portfolio.

- **Monitoring and Controlling Process Group.** Reviews performance indicators periodically for alignment with strategic objectives and verifying the benefits to the organization from the components of the portfolio.

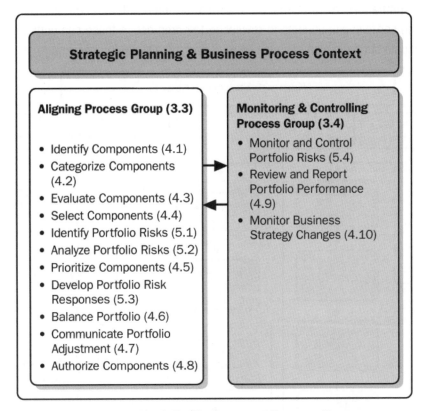

Figure 3-1: Portfolio Management Process Groups

The remainder of this chapter provides information and interlinked processes for establishing and managing a portfolio of components, details the above Process Groups, and includes the following major sections:

3.1 Portfolio Management Process Interactions

3.2 Portfolio Management Process Groups

3.3 Aligning Process Group

3.4 Monitoring and Controlling Process Group

3.1 Portfolio Management Process Interactions

There is a tight linkage between the Portfolio Management Process Groups and the ongoing business process cycle of developing a business strategy, aligning projects and programs to that strategy, and monitoring the results of these decisions.

Figure 3-2 illustrates the relationships between portfolio management processes, Process Groups, and the organization's strategic plan. The diagram illustrates:

- **The organization's strategic plan:** The decision base for any project portfolio management process and the basis for establishing the determining factors that will make each portfolio unique.

- **Portfolio management processes:** A series of interrelated processes, from identifying and authorizing portfolio components to reviewing the progress of those components. These processes accommodate strategic plan changes by revisiting the aligning processes.

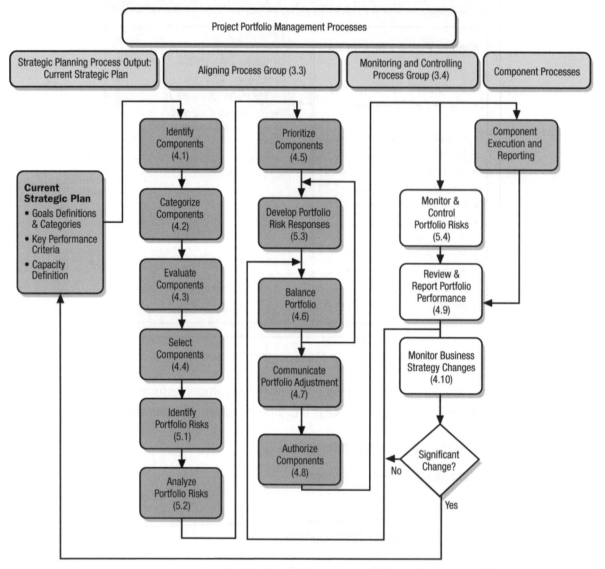

Figure 3-2. Portfolio Management Processes – High-Level Illustration

3.2 Portfolio Management Process Groups

The following sections identify and describe the Portfolio Management Process Groups. These Process Groups have clear dependencies and are typically performed in the same sequence for each portfolio. They are independent of application areas or industry focus. The portfolio management team may repeat individual Process Groups and individual constituent processes prior to component authorization.

The process flow diagram, Figure 3-2, provides an overall summary of the basic flow and interactions amongst Process Groups, strategic plan, and the project management process. A Process Group includes the constituent portfolio management processes that are linked by the respective inputs and outputs, where the result or outcome of one process becomes the input to another. The Process Groups should not to be thought of as portfolio management phases.

Table 3-1 reflects the mapping of the 14 portfolio management processes into the 2 Portfolio Management Process Groups and the 2 Portfolio Management Knowledge Areas. Each of the key portfolio management processes is shown in the Process Group in which most of the activity takes place.

Table 3-1. Mapping of the Portfolio Management Processes to the Portfolio Management Process Groups and Knowledge Areas

Portfolio Management Process Groups		
Process Knowledge Areas	**Aligning Process Group**	**Monitoring and Controlling Process Group**
Portfolio Governance	Identify Components (4.1)	Review and Report Portfolio Performance (4.9)
	Categorize Components (4.2)	Monitor Business Strategy Changes (4.10)
	Evaluate Components (4.3)	Communicate Portfolio Adjustment (4.7)
	Select Components (4.4)	
	Prioritize Components (4.5)	
	Balance Portfolio (4.6)	
	Authorize Components (4.8)	
Portfolio Risk Management	Identify Portfolio Risks (5.1)	Monitor and Control Portfolio Risks (5.4)
	Analyze Portfolio Risks (5.2)	
	Develop Portfolio Risk Responses (5.3)	

3.3 Aligning Process Group

The Aligning Process Group depends on subprocesses within the business process cycle's planning and authorization phase. The Aligning Process Group ensures the availability of information regarding the strategic goals that the portfolio is to support, as well as, operational rules for evaluating components and building the portfolio. The processes in this Process Group help establish a structured method for aligning the mix of portfolio components to the organization's strategy.

The Aligning Process Group is most active at the time the organization identifies and updates its strategic goals, near-term budgets, and plans. Traditionally, these activities take place at the annual budgeting time although some organizations have more or less frequent cycles. Such activities could be scheduled quarterly, for example, or may occur because of unscheduled changes in the business climate.

3.3.1 Identify Components

The purpose of this process is to create an up-to-date list, with sufficient information, of ongoing and new components that will be managed through portfolio management (see Figure 3-3).

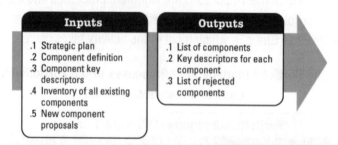

Figure 3-3. Identify Components: Inputs and Outputs

3.3.2 Categorize Components

The Categorize Components process assigns identified components to relevant business categories using a common set of decision filters and criteria for subsequent evaluation, selection, prioritization, and balancing (see Figure 3-4). The portfolio management team defines the categories on the basis of the strategic plan. The components in a given group have a common goal and can be measured on the same basis regardless of their origin in the organization. The categorization of the components allows the organization to balance its investment and its risks between all strategic categories and strategic goals.

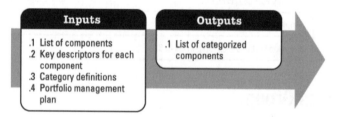

Figure 3-4. Categorize Components: Inputs and Outputs

3.3.3 Evaluate Components

Evaluate Components is the process of gathering all pertinent information to evaluate components for the purpose of comparing them to facilitate the selection process (see Figure 3-5). The portfolio management team gathers and summarizes information for each component of the portfolio. The information can be qualitative and/or quantitative and comes from a variety of sources across the organization. The portfolio management team repeats the data collection several times until the required level of completeness is achieved. Graphs, charts, documents, and recommendations are produced to support the subsequent selection process.

By its definition, project portfolio management must only select projects that align with the business strategy and meet certain criteria. Without a successful evaluation and selection process, unnecessary or poorly planned projects can come into the portfolio and increase the workload of the organization, thus hampering the benefits realized from truly important and strategic projects.

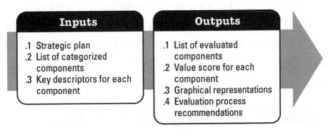

Figure 3-5. Evaluate Components: Inputs and Outputs

3.3.4   Select Components

This process is necessary to produce a subset of the organization's components worthy of pursuit based on the evaluation recommendations and the organization's selection criteria. The Select Components process produces a list of components along with required information about each component needed for prioritization. (see Figure 3-6)

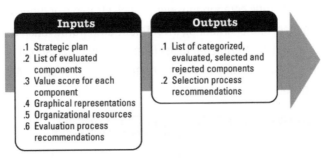

Figure 3-6. Select Components: Inputs and Outputs

3.3.5   Identify Portfolio Risks

Risk identification determines which risks could affect the portfolio and documents their characteristics (see Figure 3-7). A portfolio comprises different categories of components, so the potential impact of each category of component on risk management could be different.

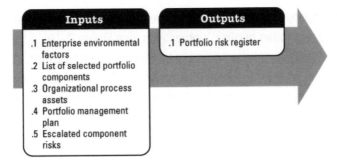

Figure 3-7. Identify Portfolio Risks: Inputs and Outputs

3.3.6 Analyze Portfolio Risks

The Analyze Portfolio Risk process includes methods for prioritizing the identified risks for further action (see Figure 3-8). Organizations can improve the portfolio's performance effectively by focusing on high-priority risks. Risk analysis determines the priority of identified risks using their probability of occurrence, the corresponding impact on portfolio objectives, such as business enhancement, return on investment, as well as other factors. The analysis also takes into account the risk tolerance of the organization and the individual stakeholders.

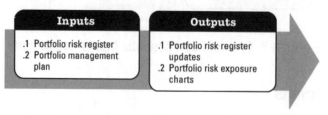

Figure 3-8. Analyze Portfolio Risks: Inputs and Outputs

3.3.7 Prioritize Components

The purpose of this process is to rank components within each strategic or funding category (e.g., innovation, cost savings, growth, maintenance, and operations), investment time frame (such as short, medium, and long-term), risk versus return profile, and organizational focus (such as customer, supplier, and internal) according to established criteria (see Figure 3-9). This step ranks the components to support subsequent analysis required to validate and balance the portfolio.

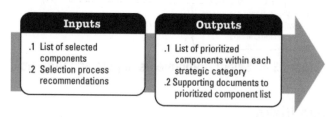

Figure 3-9. Prioritize Components: Inputs and Outputs

3.3.8 Develop Portfolio Risk Responses

Develop Portfolio Risk Responses is the process of developing options and determining actions to enhance opportunities and reduce threats to the portfolio's objectives (see Figure 3-10). It follows the Analyze Portfolio Risks process. It includes identifying and assigning responsibility to one or more persons (the "risk owner") for each agreed-upon and funded risk response. Risk response planning addresses the risks by their priority, inserting resources and activities into the budget, schedule, and portfolio management plan, as needed.

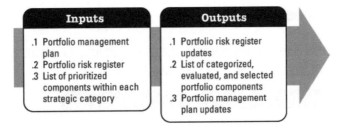

Figure 3-10. Develop Portfolio Risk Responses: Inputs and Outputs

3.3.9   Balance Portfolio

The purpose of this process is to develop the portfolio component mix with the greatest potential to support the organization's strategic initiatives and achieve strategic objectives (see Figure 3-11). Portfolio balancing supports the primary benefits of portfolio management and the ability to plan and allocate resources (such as financial, physical assets, IT assets, and human resources) according to strategic direction and the ability to maximize portfolio return within the organization's desired risk profile.

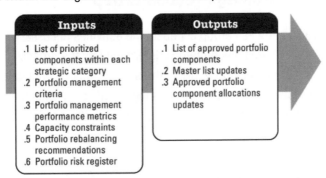

Figure 3-11. Balance Portfolio: Inputs and Outputs

3.3.10 Communicate Portfolio Adjustment

The portfolio management team communicates portfolio changes to stakeholders to set expectations and to provide a clear understanding of the impact of the change. Based on feedback, the organization can assess the impact of the changes on the organization's portfolio performance goals and the larger business strategies. The purpose of communicating portfolio adjustments is to satisfy the needs of the stakeholders, resolve issues, and ensure that the portfolio stays on track in meeting its goals (see Figure 3-12).

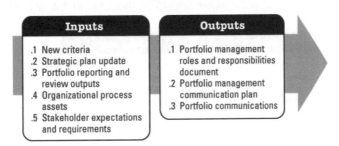

Figure 3-12. Communicate Portfolio Adjustment: Inputs and Outputs

3.3.11 Authorize Components

The purpose of this process is to formally allocate resources required to execute selected components and to formally communicate portfolio-balancing decisions (see Figure 3-13).

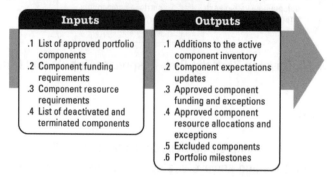

Figure 3-13. Authorize Components: Inputs and Outputs

3.4 Monitoring and Controlling Process Group

The Monitoring and Controlling Process Group conducts the activities necessary to ensure that the portfolio as a whole is performing to achieve predefined metrics determined by the organization. Metrics, such as total return on investment (ROI) or net present value (NPV) thresholds, may be monitored by category or across the entire portfolio. In some instances, the portfolio management team evaluates and tracks components of interest. The Monitoring and Controlling Process Group includes the portfolio management processes in Sections 3.4.1 through 3.4.3.

3.4.1 Monitor and Control Portfolio Risks

The Monitor and Control Portfolio Risks process applies techniques, such as variance and trend analysis, which require the use of performance data generated during component execution (see Figure 3-14). Other purposes of risk monitoring and control are to determine if:

- Portfolio assumptions are still valid,
- Risk, as assessed, has changed from its prior state,
- Proper risk management policies and procedures are being followed, and
- Contingency reserves of cost or schedule should be modified in line with the risks.

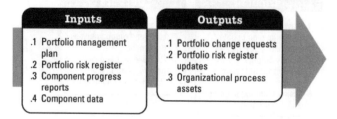

Figure 3-14. Monitor and Control Portfolio Risks

3.4.2 Review and Report Portfolio Performance

The purpose of this process is to gather and report performance indicators and review the portfolio at an appropriate predetermined frequency (see Figure 3-15). This ensures both alignment with the organizational strategy and effective resource utilization. The review cycle examines all components and is executed on a timeline that is specified by the organization. Each cycle may contain several reviews with a different focus and depth of analysis applied in each. The key performance indicators also vary for each component since the purpose of each review varies.

Ultimately, the purpose of the review process is to ensure that the portfolio contains only components that support achievement of the strategic goals. To achieve that end, the portfolio management team must add, reprioritize, or exclude components based on their performance and ongoing alignment with the defined strategy.

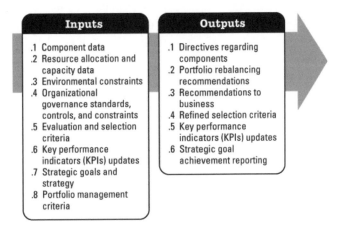

Figure 3-15. Review and Report Portfolio Performance: Inputs and Outputs

3.4.3 Monitor Business Strategy Changes

This process enables the portfolio management process to respond to changes in business strategy (see Figure 3-16). Incremental changes to the strategic plan generally do not require changes to the portfolio. However, significant changes in the business environment often result in a new strategic direction, thereby impacting the portfolio. A significant change in strategic direction will impact component categorization or prioritization and this will require rebalancing the portfolio.

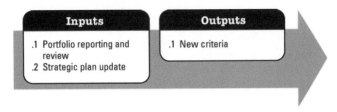

Figure 3-16. Monitor Business Strategy Changes: Inputs and Outputs

SECTION III

THE PORTFOLIO MANAGEMENT KNOWLEDGE AREAS

Chapter 4

- Portfolio Governance

Chapter 5

- Portfolio Risk Management

CHAPTER 4

PORTFOLIO GOVERNANCE

Portfolio Governance includes the processes to:

- Select and fund the investment portfolio,

- Monitor and control portfolio investments,

- Communicate decisions about the investment portfolio and constituent components within the portfolio, and

- Ensure the investment portfolio continues to align with strategic objectives.

Governance processes ensure that investment decisions are taken to identify opportunities, to select activities to fund, and to achieve performance targets.

Portfolio Governance processes are as follows:

4.1 Identify Components—Creating an up-to-date list of qualified components that will be managed through portfolio management.

4.2 Categorize Components—Organizing components into relevant business groups to which a common set of decision filters and criteria can be applied for evaluation, selection, prioritization, and balancing.

4.3 Evaluate Components—Gathering information for the review of portfolio components in preparation for the selection process.

4.4 Select Components—Developing a subset of the organization's components based on the organization's selection criteria that will be considered for further prioritization.

4.5 Prioritize Components—Ranking components within categories according to established criteria for balancing the portfolio.

4.6 Balance Portfolio—Creating the component mix with the greatest potential to collectively support the organization's strategic initiatives and achieve strategic objectives.

4.7 Communicate Portfolio Adjustment—Setting stakeholder expectations and providing a clear understanding of the impact of changes on the organization's portfolio performance goals and business strategies.

4.8 Authorize Components—Allocating resources required to develop business cases or execute selected components and to formally communicate portfolio-balancing decisions.

4.9 Review and Report Portfolio Performance—Gathering and reporting performance indicators against established criteria for success and reviewing the portfolio at an appropriate predetermined frequency to ensure alignment both with the organizational strategy and effective resource utilization.

4.10 Monitor Business Strategy Changes—Maintaining an awareness of changes in the business strategy to enable the portfolio management process to respond accordingly.

These processes interact with each other and with the processes in the other Knowledge Area. Each process will involve effort from one or more persons or groups of persons based on the needs of the process and portfolio. Each process occurs at least once during every portfolio review cycle and is likely to occur several times during each year, depending on the number of review cycles conducted. Although the processes are presented here as discrete elements with well-defined interfaces, in practice they may overlap and interact in ways not detailed in this document. Process interactions are discussed in detail in Chapter 3 (see Figures 4-1 and 4-2).

Portfolio Governance

4.1 Identify Components

.1 Inputs
  .1 Strategic plan
  .2 Component definition
  .3 Component key descriptors
  .4 Inventory of all existing components
  .5 New component proposals
.2 Tools & Techniques
  .1 Documentation of all inventoried components based on key descriptors
  .2 Comparison of all inventoried components with component definition
  .3 Identification of components
  .4 Expert judgment
.3 Outputs
  .1 List of components
  .2 Key descriptors for each component
  .3 List of rejected components

4.5 Prioritize Components

.1 Inputs
  .1 List of selected components
  .2 Selection process recommendations
.2 Tools & Techniques
  .1 Weighted ranking
  .2 Scoring techniques
  .3 Expert judgment
.3 Outputs
  .1 List of prioritized components within each strategic category
  .2 Supporting documents to prioritized component list

4.10 Monitor Business Strategy Changes

.1 Inputs
  .1 Portfolio reporting and review
  .2 Strategic plan update
.2 Tools & Techniques
  .1 Expert judgment
  .2 Criteria re-weighting
  .3 Graphical representations
.3 Outputs
  .1 New criteria

4.2 Categorize Components

.1 Inputs
  .1 List of components
  .2 Key descriptors for each component
  .3 Category definitions
.2 Tools & Techniques
  .1 Categorization of components
  .2 Expert judgment
.3 Outputs
  .1 List of categorized components

4.6 Balance Portfolio

.1 Inputs
  .1 List of prioritized components within each strategic category
  .2 Portfolio management criteria
  .3 Portfolio management performance metrics
  .4 Capacity constraints
  .5 Portfolio rebalancing recommendations from reporting and review
  .6 Portfolio risk register
.2 Tools & Techniques
  .1 Cost benefit analysis
  .2 Quantitative analysis
  .3 Scenario analysis
  .4 Probability analysis
  .5 Graphical analytical methods
  .6 Expert judgment
.3 Outputs
  .1 List of approved portfolio components
  .2 Master list of updates
  .3 Approved portfolio component allocation updates

4.7 Communicate Portfolio Adjustment

.1 Inputs
  .1 New criteria
  .2 Strategic plan update
  .3 Portfolio reporting and review outputs
  .4 Organizational process assets
  .5 Stakeholder expectations and requirements
.2 Tools & Techniques
  .1 Communication requirements analysis
.3 Outputs
  .1 Portfolio management roles and responsibilities document
  .2 Portfolio management communication plan
  .3 Portfolio communications

4.3 Evaluate Components

.1 Inputs
  .1 Strategic plan
  .2 List of categorized components
  .3 Key descriptors for each component
.2 Tools & Techniques
  .1 Scoring model comprising weighted key criteria
  .2 Graphical representations
  .3 Expert judgment
.3 Outputs
  .1 List of evaluated components
  .2 Value score for each component
  .3 Graphical representations
  .4 Evaluation process recommendations

4.8 Authorize Components

.1 Inputs
  .1 List of approved portfolio components
  .2 Component funding requirements
  .3 Component resource requirements
  .4 List of deactivated and terminated components
.2 Tools & Techniques
  .1 Portfolio management roles and responsibilities document
  .2 Portfolio management communication plan
  .3 Portfolio authorization process
.3 Outputs
  .1 Additions to the active component inventory
  .2 Component expectations updates
  .3 Approved component funding and exceptions
  .4 Approved component resource allocations and exceptions
  .5 Excluded components
  .6 Portfolio milestones

4.4 Select Components

.1 Inputs
  .1 Strategic plan
  .2 List of evaluated components
  .3 Value score for each component
  .4 Graphical representations
  .5 Organizational resources
  .6 Evaluation process recommendations
.2 Tools & Techniques
  .1 Human resource capacity analyses
  .2 Financial capacity analyses
  .3 Asset capacity analyses
  .4 Expert judgment
.3 Outputs
  .1 List of categorized, evaluated, selected, and rejected components
  .2 Selection process recommendations

4.9 Review and Report Portfolio Performance

.1 Inputs
  .1 Component data
  .2 Resource allocation and capacity data
  .3 Environmental constraints
  .4 Organizational governance standards, controls, and constraints
  .5 Evaluation and selection criteria
  .6 Key performance indicators (KPIs) updates
  .7 Strategic goals and strategy
  .8 Portfolio management criteria
.2 Tools & Techniques
  .1 Project/portfolio management system
  .2 Financial reporting systems
  .3 Performance measurement techniques
  .4 Graphical representations
  .5 Portfolio management resources
  .6 Portfolio management performance variance/ alert techniques
.3 Outputs
  .1 Directives regarding components
  .2 Portfolio rebalancing recommendations
  .3 Recommendations to business
  .4 Refined selection criteria
  .5 Key performance indicators (KPIs) updates
  .6 Strategic goal achievement reporting

Figure 4-1. Portfolio Governance Overview

The basic approach to Project Portfolio Governance described in this chapter is intended to provide a step-by-step framework to manage a portfolio of components to realize benefits and maximize value for the organization. The processes covered are recognized as generally accepted practices for most project portfolios most of the time, enhancing the probability of success over time. However, each portfolio management team should always determine the process appropriate for a given organization and the appropriate degree of rigor for each process. Therefore, the actual project portfolio management process implemented will vary from one organization to the next.

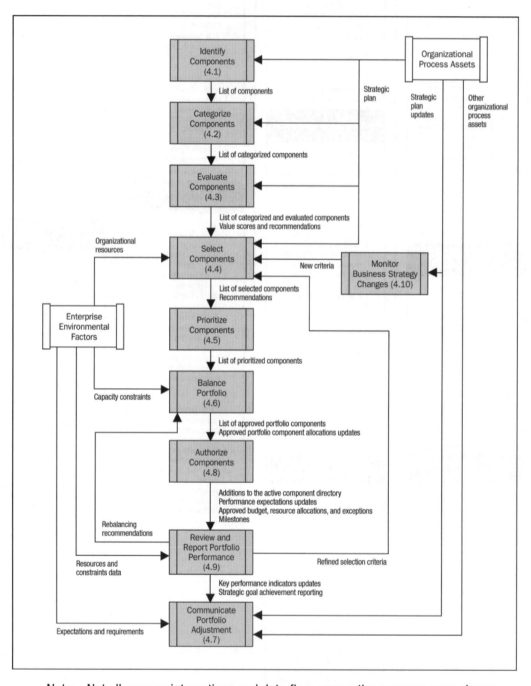

Note—Not all process interactions and data flow among the processes are shown.

Figure 4-2. Portfolio Governance Process Flow Diagram

4.1 Identify Components

The purpose of identifying qualified components is to maintain a list of portfolio components that are relevant to a specific portfolio, with sufficient information to enable them to be managed (see Figure 4-3).

Key activities include the following:

- Evaluating ongoing components and new components proposals against pre-determined portfolio and component definitions and related key descriptors.

- Rejecting components that do not fit within the predetermined definition(s); and

- Classifying identified components into predefined classes, such as project, program, portfolio, and other works.

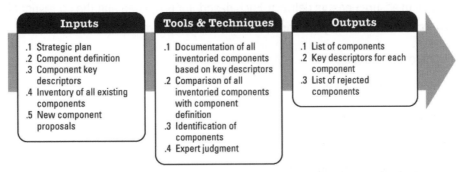

Figure 4-3. Identify Components: Inputs, Tools & Techniques, and Outputs

4.1.1 Identify Components: Inputs

.1 Strategic Plan

An organization uses a strategic plan to align its organizational and financial structure with organizational priorities, mission, and objectives. A strategic plan typically includes a vision and a mission statement, a description of the organization's long-term goals, objectives, and means by which the organization plans to achieve these general goals and objectives. The strategic plan may also identify external factors that might affect achievement of long-term goals. Strategic planning is a process used by an organization to anticipate and adapt to expected changes. Management develops operational plans to support the annual or ongoing operations of the organization. These plans may be loosely or tightly integrated with the organization's strategic plan.

.2 Component Definition

The component definition is based on the strategic and/or operational plans' goals and objectives. The component definition will be useful to make a first screening on the component list. For example, to be part of the portfolio, a component should be greater than a predetermined minimum size and be in line with the basic strategic objectives. Some examples of component definition may include, but are not limited to:

- Alignment for strategy,

- Class for component,

- Size (e.g. budget, resources).

- Duration.

- Impact for benefit,

- Impact for risk, and

- Urgency.

.3 Component Key Descriptors

The component key descriptors are used for categorizing, evaluating, and selecting components through the portfolio. The key descriptors also provide context for monitoring and controlling component performance to ensure benefits delivery. Each descriptor is defined and the corresponding acceptance levels are predetermined. Key descriptors may include, but are not limited to:

- Component number,

- Component description,

- Class of component,

- High-level plan,

- Strategic objectives supported,

- Quantitative benefits,

- Qualitative benefits,

- Component customer,

- Component sponsor,

- Key stakeholders, and

- Resources required.

.4 Inventory of All Existing Components

The inventory of all ongoing components is a list of components from previous portfolio cycles that were either authorized and are being executed through the project or program management process, or were put on a waiting list.

.5 New Component Proposals

The compilation of all new component proposals submitted since the previous portfolio cycle. The portfolio cycle may include new proposals as part of the review process to ensure that the portfolio contains the appropriate components to support achievement of the strategic goals.

4.1.2 Identify Components: Tools and Techniques

Tools and techniques for component identification help the organization produce a list of components characterized by a common set of key descriptors for further comparison, evaluation, and selection. Some of those key descriptors can also be used as preliminary filters, permitting the acceptance or rejection of components for further evaluation and implementation.

At this stage of the portfolio management process, available tools and techniques include:

.1 Documentation of All Inventoried Components Based on Key Descriptors

The sponsor of a component uses a standard set of key descriptors when providing a proposal for a new component or a change to an existing component. The key descriptors ensure that all components are comparable. Some descriptors may be used for filtering or eliminating new components, by having associated acceptance levels.

.2 Comparisons of All Inventoried Components with Component Definition

A preliminary comparison of all inventoried components against the component definition is used to identify components that meet requirements for consideration. As mentioned in Section 4.1.1.2, the component definition is used to make a first screening on the component list. For example, to be part of the portfolio, a component should be greater than a predetermined minimum size and be in line with the basic strategic objectives.

.3 Identification of Components

The identification of qualified components determines whether or not a particular component qualifies to be part of the portfolio in question.

.4 Expert Judgment

Expert judgment is often used to identify the components. Such judgment and expertise can be applied to any technical and management details during this process.

4.1.3 Identify Components: Outputs

.1 List of Components

The list of components comprises all the qualifying components meeting the definition as identified in Section 4.1.1.2, complete with appropriate documentation. This may include a list of relationships among various components.

.2 Key Descriptors for Each Component

The key descriptors for each component represent the complete documentation for each qualifying component presented on proper templates.

.3 List of Rejected Components

The list of rejected components comprises all components that do not meet the component definition or that are not correctly and completely documented. As mentioned in Section 4.1.1.2, the component definition is used to make a first screening on the component list. For example, to be part of the portfolio, a component should be greater than a predetermined minimum size and be in line with the basic strategic objectives. The portfolio management team may eliminate, rewrite, or regroup these component proposals for submission to the portfolio (or to another) process.

4.2 Categorize Components

Categorize Components involves assigning components to relevant categories to which a common set of decision filters and criteria can be applied for evaluation, selection, prioritization, and balancing (see Figure 4-4). The categories are defined on the basis of the strategic plan. The components in a given category have a common goal and can be measured on the same basis, regardless of their origin in the organization. The categorization of the components allows the organization to balance its investment and its risks between all strategic categories and strategic goals.

Key activities include:

- Identify relevant strategic categories used to categorize relevant components based on the strategic plan,

- Comparing identified components to the categorization criteria, and

- Grouping each component into only one category.

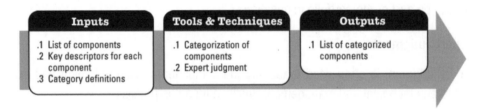

Inputs	Tools & Techniques	Outputs
.1 List of components .2 Key descriptors for each component .3 Category definitions	.1 Categorization of components .2 Expert judgment	.1 List of categorized components

Figure 4-4. Categorize Components: Inputs, Tools & Techniques, and Outputs

4.2.1 Categorize Components: Inputs

.1 List of Components

Described in Section 4.1.3.1.

.2 Key Descriptors for Each Component

Described in Section 4.1.3.2.

.3 Category Definitions

The strategic plan (Section 4.1.1.1) is used by the organization to align its organizational and budget structure with organizational priorities, missions, and objectives.

Component categories group components possessing common strategic goals and measurement criteria. The organization's executives and portfolio management team use the strategic plan to determine component categories. Categories originating from various departments or business units of the organization may also be included. The categories need to be defined and widely understood throughout the organization; they may change or evolve if the strategic plan changes or evolves. The number of categories is usually limited, examples include:

- Increased profitability (revenue increase, generation, cost reduction),
- Risk reduction,
- Efficiency improvement,
- Legal/regulatory obligation,
- Market share increase,
- Process improvement,
- Continuous improvement,
- Foundational (e.g., investments that build the infrastructure to grow the business), and
- Business imperatives (e.g., internal toolkit, IT compatibility, or upgrades).

Each category may also include subcategories to generate comparative tables, graphs, or charts, such as:

- Size (e.g., effort, budget, resources),
- Duration,
- Level of attractiveness to customers, such as basic "must-haves," that have performance differentiation in the market and exciting/hot/premium components,
- Component type (e.g., projects, programs, other work), and
- Phase.

.4 Portfolio Management Plan

The portfolio management plan is the equivalent of the master project plan as defined in the *PMBOK®Guide* – Fourth Edition and represents the collection of plans for managing the portfolio.

4.2.2 Categorize Components: Tools and Techniques

Tools and techniques for component categorization help the organization to facilitate component evaluation by assigning them to predetermined categories. This helps to compare components that address similar organizational needs and/or strategic concerns. It also facilitates portfolio balancing later on, by ensuring that components are selected and managed within a set of categories addressing all of the strategic objectives of the organization.

At this stage of the portfolio management process, available tools and techniques include:

.1 Categorization of Components

Each identified component along with the key descriptors is compared to the categorization criteria and is assigned to a given category for the purpose of comparing, evaluating, measuring, and selecting between similar components.

.2 Expert Judgment

The portfolio management team often uses expert judgment to assess the inputs needed to categorize the components. Such judgment and expertise is applied to any technical and management details during this process.

4.2.3 Categorize Components: Outputs

.1 List of Categorized Components

The result is a list of components grouped by category, comprising all identified components divided within all the strategic categories. When a component cannot be categorized, it is up to the portfolio management group to decide whether to keep it on the list for further evaluation and selection.

4.3 Evaluate Components

Components are evaluated to provide comparisons in order to facilitate the selection process (see Figure 4-5). All pertinent information is gathered and summarized for each component of the portfolio. The information can be qualitative and/or quantitative and comes from a variety of sources across the organization. The portfolio management team may revise the data several times until reaching the required level of completeness. Graphs, charts, documents, and recommendations support the subsequent selection process.

Key activities within this process include:

- Evaluating components with a scoring model comprising weighted key criteria,
- Producing graphical representations to facilitate decision making in the selection process, and
- Making recommendations for the selection process.

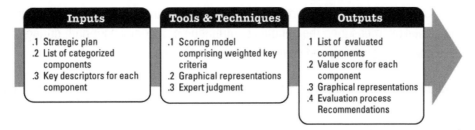

Figure 4-5. Evaluate Components: Inputs, Tools & Techniques, and Outputs

4.3.1   Evaluate Components: Inputs

.1   Strategic Plan

Described in Section 4.1.1.1.

.2   List of Categorized Components

Described in Section 4.2.3.1.

.3   Key Descriptors for Each Component

Described in Section 4.1.3.2.

4.3.2   Evaluate Components: Tools and Techniques

The evaluation step is an enabler for the portfolio selection as it makes components comparable. Therefore, tools and techniques for evaluation allow the comparing of components in the portfolio based on carefully selected criteria.

The portfolio management team can apply a series of evaluation criteria associated with various business aspects. These criteria should enable the measurement of the contribution of the component to strategic business objectives and could allow for tracking the benefits contribution expected from the component.

Some examples of evaluation criteria may include, but are not limited to:

- General business criteria,
- Financial criteria,
- Risk-related criteria,
- Legal/regulatory compliance criteria,
- Human resources (HR)-related criteria,
- Marketing criteria, and
- Technical criteria.

It is important to select evaluation criteria which best support the achievement of strategic objectives. Such criteria will also allow measuring the benefits contribution of a component both during the steps of the alignment process and the monitoring and controlling Process Groups.

At this stage of the portfolio management process, available tools and techniques that can be used include, among others:

.1 Scoring Model Comprising Weighted Key Criteria

Scoring models constitute one possible method used to evaluate components and make them comparable. As illustrated in Figure 4-6, a scoring model consists of a series of evaluation criteria having a weight expressed as a percentage and a score. The weight for each criterion is expressed in percentages (that in total must add up to 100%) and determines the relative importance of each criterion in the component evaluation. The score applies to each criterion and should be discriminating (such as 0, 5, and 10). The score measures if each criterion is met or not. Each score level must be clearly defined to ensure consistent evaluation from component to component. The score multiplied by the weight provides a value for each criterion and the total of all these criteria values is the total value of the component.

SCORING MODEL		Evaluation					
List of Criteria	**Weight**	**Low**	**Medium**	**High**	**Score**	**Total**	
Criteria 1	20%	0	5	10	10	2	
Criteria 2	20%	0	5	10	10	2	Indicator "Y"
Criteria 3	10%	0	5	10	5	0.5	
Criteria 4	15%	0	5	10	10	1.5	
Criteria 5	5%	0	5	10	5	0.25	
Criteria 6	5%	0	5	10	0	0	
Criteria 7	5%	0	5	10	10	0.5	
Criteria 8	5%	0	5	10	5	0.25	Indicator "X"
Criteria 9	10%	0	5	10	0	0	
Criteria 10	5%	0	5	10	5	0.25	
TOTAL WEIGHT = 100%				**TOTAL SCORE**		7.25	
				Indicator "Y" (0 to 1)		0.83	
				Indicator "X" (0 to 1)		0.4	

Figure 4-6. Multi-Criteria Scoring Model

A typical scoring model can be effectively designed and used by following these steps:

- Establish a list of criteria in alignment with business objectives or;

- Define groups of criteria, if and whenever possible, to build specific key indicators that need more than one criterion to be properly evaluated (e.g., criteria 1 to 6 = Indicator "Y") or;

- Establish relative weights among the criteria;

- Determine the evaluation scoring model to be used, for example:
    ○ -0, 5, 10,
    ○ -1 to 10, or
    ○ -1 to 5.
- Provide scoring guidance for each rating in the scoring model;
- Evaluate the component(s) against each criterion;
- Multiply the evaluation by the weight to get a total per criterion;
- Add the totals for each criterion to get the total score for the component(s); and
- Compare component results.

Criteria, which represent mandates, such as regulatory or operational requirements, and must be fulfilled, deserve particular attention. Components which are required to comply with such mandates need to be earmarked to assure their inclusion in the final portfolio.

.2 Graphical Representations

Various graphical representations may also be used to facilitate comparisons between the components being evaluated. Graphical representations include such things as histograms, pie charts, line charts, and bubble charts. Two-criterion comparison grids, like the example illustrated in Figure 4-7, are among the most utilized and effective graphical tools to compare components that must meet more than one selection criterion. A typical pair of criteria used by organizations is benefits (Criterion 1) vs. strategic alignment (Criterion 2).

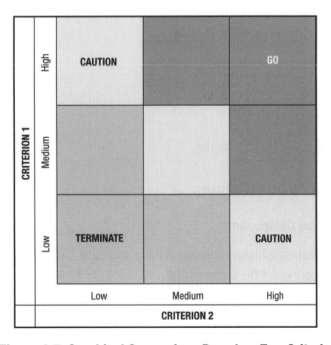

Figure 4-7. Graphical Comparison Based on Two Criteria

One can effectively design and use a two-criterion comparison grid by using the following implementation steps:

- Choose two criteria,

- Evaluate each component against each criterion,

- Position each component in the grid, for example, for component XYZ: Criterion 1= medium and Criterion 2=medium,

- Components evaluated HIGH have a high score,

- Components evaluated LOW have a low score, and

- The grid can be color-coded to indicate which combinations of criteria values are preferred by the organization and which are to be avoided, for example:

  o Components positioned in the "red zone" (Terminate) have low value for the organization, and

  o Components positioned in the "green zone" (Go) have high value for the organization.

Graphical representations are usually done to compare components only within the same category, in order to prevent comparing components that do not address similar organizational concerns and/ or objectives.

.3 Expert Judgment

The portfolio management team often uses expert judgment to assess the inputs needed to compare the components and to apply it to any technical and management details during this process.

The portfolio management team also applies expert judgment to identify relationships between components which are under consideration. Such relationships may be independent components or components coupled together which include:

- Dependencies,

- Redundancies,

- Partial overlap, and

- Mutual exclusivity of components.

4.3.3 Evaluate Components: Outputs

.1 List of Evaluated Components

A list of evaluated components is produced and approved for each category. Components can be compared by category or for the entire portfolio.

.2 Value Score for Each Component

A total value score is calculated with the scoring model for each component.

.3 Graphical Representations

The portfolio management team produces a number of graphical representations (e.g., scoring matrices and bubble charts) to support decision making.

.4 Evaluation Process Recommendations

The portfolio management team makes recommendations to the portfolio management board at the end of the evaluation process. The portfolio management team can make recommendations for a component, a category, or the entire portfolio, based on the value of each component or a group of components.

4.4 Select Components

This process is necessary to produce a subset of the organization's components based on the evaluation process recommendations and the organization's selection criteria (see Figure 4-8). The evaluation determines the value of each component and produces a list of components that are ready for prioritization.

Key activities within this process include:

- Comparing components to selection criteria,

- Selecting components based on the evaluation results, and

- Producing a list of components for prioritization.

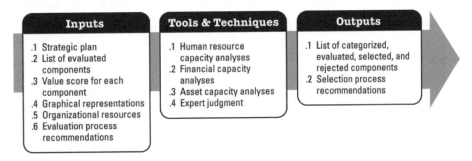

Figure 4-8. Select Components: Inputs, Tools & Techniques, and Outputs

4.4.1 Select Components: Inputs

.1 Strategic Plan

Described in Section 4.1.1.1.

.2 List of Evaluated Components

Described in Section 4.3.3.1.

.3 Value Score for Each Component

Described in Section 4.3.3.2.

.4 Graphical Representations

Described in Section 4.3.3.3.

.5 Organizational Resources

Organizational resources may include internal or external human resources, financial resources, equipment, and other assets.

.6 Evaluation Process Recommendations

Described in Section 4.3.3.4.

4.4.2 Select Components: Tools and Techniques

The organization can use tools and techniques to create a short list of components that will be considered for further prioritization. This might include using the results of the scoring model to eliminate those components not meeting acceptance threshold scores with respect to one or several predetermined criteria and/or indicators. Although this process focuses on the value of individual components, the capacity analyses will also constrain the extent of the components in the portfolio to organizational capacity constraints.

The portfolio management team applies available tools and techniques to ensure that the most desirable components are selected for inclusion in the portfolio. Some of these may include:

.1 Human Resource Capacity Analyses

The portfolio management team must conduct a human resource capacity analysis to understand the capacity of the organization to source and execute the selected projects. The portfolio management team should perform the analysis on organizational skill sets to determine the constraint generated by certain skill-set limitations. Internal resource capacity must be measured and external resource availability must be established to complete the picture. The human resource capacity will be a limiting factor for the number of projects or the size of projects the organization can execute.

.2 Financial Capacity Analyses

The portfolio management team must conduct a financial resource capacity analysis to understand the capacity of the organization to finance the selected projects. The analysis must be done through the financial and/or budget process of the organization. Internal financial capacity must be measured and external financial resource availability must be established to have a complete picture. The financial resource capacity will be a constraining factor for the number of projects or the size of projects the organization can execute. Financial capacity interacts with human resource capacity analysis and asset capacity analysis including the potential for training budgets, hiring outside resources, and make or buy decisions.

.3 Asset Capacity Analyses

An asset resource capacity analysis must be conducted to understand the physical needs of the organization to support the selected projects. The analysis must be done by type of assets (equipment, buildings, etc.) to understand the constraint generated by certain asset limitations. The asset capacity will be a limiting factor for the number of projects and the size of projects the organization can execute.

.4 Expert Judgment

The portfolio management team often uses expert judgment to assess the inputs needed to select the components. The portfolio management team uses expert judgment to assign a component score which will provide a foundation for determining the list of components that will be selected for prioritization and balancing. The portfolio management team applies such judgment and expertise to any technical and management details during this process.

4.4.3 Select Components: Outputs

.1 List of Categorized, Evaluated, Selected, and Rejected Components

A list of evaluated components approved for further analysis is produced. Components can be compared by category or for the entire portfolio.

.2 Selection Process Recommendations

Recommendations are made at the end of the selection process. The recommendations can be made for a component, a category or the entire portfolio. These recommendations can include prioritization, component segmentation, and acceptance or rejection of a component.

4.5 Prioritize Components

The prioritization process enables an organization to objectively compare each component against all other selected components, using criteria defined by the organization (see Figure 4-9). The prioritization process generates information that will be used by the organization to decide which of the components can be accommodated by the organization's financial, human, and technological resources, as well as the organization's ability to assimilate organizational change. The prioritization of portfolio components is a prerequisite activity for balancing the portfolio.

Key activities include:

- Confirming the classification of components in accordance with predetermined strategic categories,
- Assigning scoring or weighting criteria for ranking components, and
- Determining which components should receive highest priority within the portfolio.

Figure 4-9. Prioritize Components: Inputs, Tools & Techniques, and Outputs

4.5.1 Prioritize Components: Inputs

.1 List of Selected Components

Described in Section 4.4.3.1.

.2 Selection Process Recommendations

Described in Section 4.4.3.2.

4.5.2 Prioritize Components: Tools and Techniques

Tools and techniques for component prioritization are designed to assist members of the organization in their prioritization of portfolio components. The criteria might be the same as used in the scoring model to evaluate and select components. For prioritization, the components will be compared to separate and combined entities in an effort to prioritize them in a coherent way to ensure the optimal alignment with the strategic plan.

.1 Weighted Ranking

This is the process of ranking components within each category based on values assigned. Components are ranked according to pre-established criteria as illustrated in Figures 4-10 and 4-11.

	PROJECT A	PROJECT B	PROJECT C	PROJECT D	PROJECT E	PROJECT F	RANK	
PROJECT A		1	1	1	1	1	5	First Priority
PROJECT B	0		0	1	1	0	2	
PROJECT C	0	1		1	1	0	3	
PROJECT D	0	0	0		1	0	1	
PROJECT E	0	0	0	0		0	0	Last Priority
PROJECT F	0	1	1	1	1		4	

Figure 4-10. Single Criterion Prioritization Model

The single criterion approach, as illustrated in Figure 4-10, is usually a pair-wise comparison of different projects with one another, to rank them hierarchically from the one that should be given the highest priority to the one(s) that should not be undertaken within a given portfolio cycle. In the example presented in Figure 4-10, each project is compared to each of the others, then scored and prioritized using the following steps:

- If Project A has more value than Project B, score 1,

- If Project B has less value than Project C, score 0,

- Add scores horizontally for each project, and

- The project with the highest score becomes the first priority.

PROJECTS	Criterion 1		Criterion 2 * Probability of Success		Criterion 3		Criterion 4		PRIORITY	
	Measure	Rank	Result	Rank	Level of Importance	Rank	Measure	Rank	Score	Priority
Project 1	16.0	2	8.8 ($11M X 80%)	2	5 (++)	1	$2M	1	1.50	1
Project 3	14.0	4	18.9 ($21M X 90%)	1	4	2	$2.5M	2	2.25	2
Project 4	15.5	3	8.45 ($13M X 65%)	3	2	4	$3M	3	3.25	3
Project 2	19.0	1	5.95 ($7M X 85%)	4	1 (--)	6	$4.3M	4	3.75	4
Project 5	10.0	6	5.4 ($6M X 90%)	5	3	3	$5.2M	6	5.00	5
Project 6	12.0	5	2.1 ($3M X 70%)	6	1.5	5	$4.6M	5	5.25	6

Figure 4-11. Multiple-Criteria Weighted Ranking

A multiple criterion model for weighted ranking, as the one illustrated in Figure 4-11, can be designed and used effectively by using the following steps:

- Choose a set of evaluation criteria,

- Measure each project for each criterion,

- Rank projects for each criterion,

- For each project, add the rank number and divide by the number of criteria measured to produce the score, and

- Determine the priority based on the score (the lowest score giving the highest priority).

.2 Scoring Techniques

The numerical methods that are used to consolidate ranked components within each category are shown in Figure 4-11.

.3 Expert Judgment

Expert judgment is often used to assess the inputs needed to determine how to prioritize components. Such judgment and expertise is applied to any technical and management details during this process.

4.5.3 Prioritize Components: Outputs

.1 List of Prioritized Components within Each Strategic Category

This list is the prioritized list of components for portfolio balancing along with appropriate documentation.

.2 Supporting Documents to Prioritized Component List

In portfolio balancing, these are the documents that support the prioritized list of components within each strategic category.

4.6 Balance Portfolio

Portfolio balancing provides the component mix with the greatest potential to collectively support the organization's strategic initiatives and achieve strategic objectives. Portfolio balancing supports the ability to plan and allocate resources according to strategic direction and the ability to maximize portfolio return within the organization's predefined desired risk profile (see Figure 4-12).

Portfolio balancing also includes the evaluation and management of trade-offs of objectives, such as the management of risk and return, balancing short-term goals against long-term goals and balancing technologies and project types to align with the strategic business objectives. Investments of limited resources are also balanced across the portfolio to reflect strategic priorities. Components that deliver a lower level of benefit are removed from the portfolio to allow the organization to focus resources on higher priorities.

Balancing also incorporates groupings of components with cross dependencies to ensure that a high-priority component includes all of the dependencies, including costs and benefits for the entire group. The portfolio baseline is set to monitor costs and benefits through later stages, and to re-balance as needed. Balancing of activities involves reviewing selected and prioritized portfolio components. The portfolio is then balanced to support established strategic objectives using predefined portfolio management criteria, the organization's desired risk profile, portfolio performance metrics, and capacity constraints. A recommendation for either maintaining the portfolio "as is" or adjusting the portfolio is issued at completion of the balancing activities. In essence, this process includes:

- Adding new components that have been selected and prioritized for authorization;
- Identifying components that are not authorized based on the review process; and
- Identifying components to be suspended, reprioritized, or terminated based on the review process.

Using a decision matrix, part of the organizational process assets, can help portfolio balancing. For example, a decision matrix for the following types of infrastructure-related components might include:

- Systems that satisfy a significant portion of the business delivering high quality service,

- Applications that increase the value of components or leverage business processes,

- Applications that automate declining or irreplaceable skills,

- Applications that decrease in value because the components are technically weak, and

- Relationships and dependencies with existing portfolio components.

In order for the portfolio to achieve a desired return while still complying with the established portfolio management criteria, the selection mix of components should also take into account similarities and synergies that exist between components. Enhancing these interconnections fully leverages all aspects of the portfolio to generate the greatest return with the minimum investment.

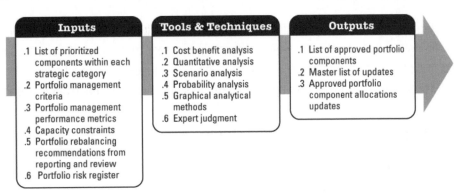

Figure 4-12. Balance Portfolio: Inputs, Tools & Techniques, and Outputs

4.6.1 Balance Portfolio: Inputs

.1 List of Prioritized Components within Each Strategic Category

Described in 4.5.3.1. The prioritized list of components is provided for portfolio balancing.

.2 Portfolio Management Criteria

Specific objectives, constraints and/or guidelines for use by the portfolio manager when creating and managing the portfolio are identified. Examples may include investment diversification objectives as dictated by evolving business direction, risk tolerance thresholds as market conditions change, and financial return.

.3 Portfolio Management Performance Metrics

Metrics and performance goals established by the organization to assess portfolio performance and to determine whether the portfolio is performing as planned or if portfolio adjustments are needed. Examples of metrics include portfolio return, risk, diversification, etc.

.4 Capacity Constraints

Capacity constraints include the organization's financial, physical assets, and human resource constraints by category.

.5 Portfolio Rebalancing Recommendations

Periodically an output of the review process will be a recommendation to terminate or realign existing portfolio components. Consequently the reporting and review process would invoke the portfolio balancing process to ensure that any changes to the portfolio will increase support of and improve the probability of achieving strategic goals and objectives.

.6 Portfolio Risk Register

The risk register is first developed in the Identify Portfolio Risks process and is updated during the Analyze Portfolio Risks process.

Important inputs to Develop Portfolio Risk Responses include the relative rating or priority listing of portfolio risks, a list of risks requiring response in the near term, a list of risks requiring additional analysis and response, trends in risk analysis results, root causes, risks grouped by categories, lists of potential responses, risk owners, symptoms, warning signs, and a watch list of low-priority risks.

4.6.2 Balance Portfolio: Tools and Techniques

Tools and techniques for portfolio balancing help the organization to effectively select and implement a portfolio with the best overall alignment to the strategic plan.

Portfolio components can be balanced with one another, usually within the same category (categorization also being an attempt to balance components to address all of the diverse concerns and objectives of the organization), using a variety of qualitative and quantitative methods and software tools to support the decision-making process and to allocate budget.

It is important to balance the portfolio with respect to the diverse goals of the organization such as financial organizational development and operation performance goals.

Tools and techniques include, among others:

.1 Cost Benefit Analysis

Any financial analytical method preferred by the organization. These methods may include: Net Present Value (NPV), Discounted Cash Flow (DCF), Internal Rate of Return (IRR), cost benefit ratio, payback, and options analysis.

.2 Quantitative Analysis

Quantitative analysis may include the use of spreadsheets or other tools to examine factors of interest, such as resource loading requirements over time or cash flow.

.3 Scenario Analysis

This analytical method enables decision makers to create a variety of portfolio scenarios using different combinations of both potential components and current components and evaluating their possible outcomes based on various assumptions. The analysis can be further enhanced by incorporating numerous baselines.

.4 Probability Analysis

These methods may include decision trees, flowcharts, and Monte Carlo simulation. Components are evaluated using success and failure probabilities for estimated cost, anticipated revenues, risk, and other criteria.

.5 Graphical Analytical Methods

These are graphical methods such as risk vs. return charts, histograms, pie charts, and other methods to visualize the portfolio. The next two figures illustrate two of the graphical representations often used by organizations to balance and monitor their portfolios.

Figure 4-13 presents a typical bubble graph that helps compare and balance portfolio components according to some pre-established "balancing and monitoring" criteria. Considering time issues with portfolio funding alternatives will provide the best combination of costs and risks. A bubble graph uses indicators from the scoring model or new indicators concerned with portfolio balance:

- Each bubble is a project,
- Bubble size often represents an additional variable such as cost or net present value, and
- Bubble color may refer to a specific category or any other qualitative criterion required to measure balance.

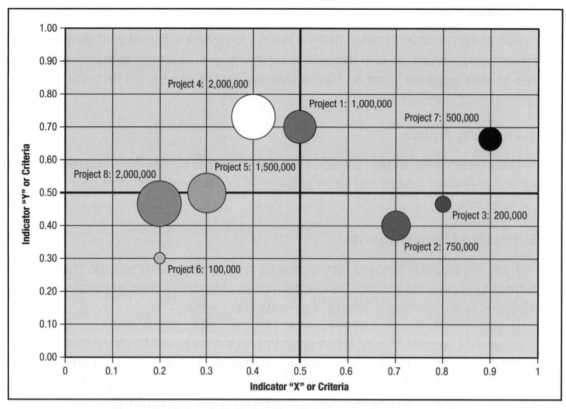

Figure 4-13. Portfolio Balancing Using Indicators or Criteria

Figure 4-14 illustrates another variant of the bubble graph, displaying portfolio components according to the category they belong to and the business unit impacted/targeted by the component. The bubble graph also uses other indicators from the scoring model or new indicators concerned with portfolio balance wherein each bubble is a project and the size of the bubble represents an additional variable, such as cost or net present value. The color of a bubble might refer to a specific qualitative criteria required to measure balance.

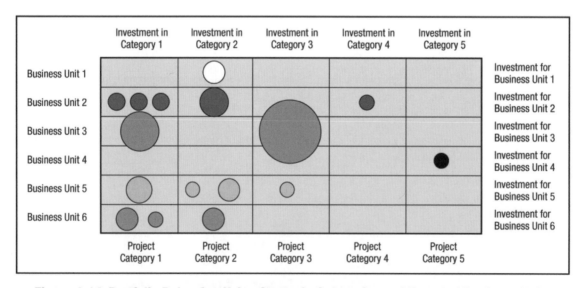

Figure 4-14. Portfolio Balancing Using Strategic Categories and Targeted Business Units

.6 Expert Judgment

The portfolio management team often uses expert judgment to assess the inputs needed to determine how to balance the portfolio. Such judgment and expertise are applied to any technical and management details during this process.

4.6.3 Balance Portfolio: Outputs

.1 List of Approved Portfolio Components

An approved portfolio component listing is the complete list of components that have been approved for execution as planned.

.2 Master List of Updates

The updated master list is a compilation of all approved, deactivated, and terminated components with the appropriate status for each. The rationale for the decision to remove a component from the portfolio or not include a component within must be added to the master list and these assessments are done on a regular basis.

.3 Approved Portfolio Component Allocations Updates

Component budget and resource approvals or exceptions should be updated on the master list. This is an iterative process that takes into account both internal and external factors that change the costs, risks, or values of the portfolio components.

4.7 Communicate Portfolio Adjustment

Changes to the portfolio are communicated to stakeholders to set expectations and provide a clear understanding of the impact of the changes on the organization's portfolio performance goals and business strategies. The purpose of communicating portfolio adjustments is to satisfy the needs of the stakeholders, resolve issues, and surface issues for resolution. Stakeholders have the ability to influence decisions.

In order to achieve the goals of the portfolio, the portfolio management team must understand the requirements of stakeholders and meet their informational needs. This includes stakeholders with conflicting goals and those competing for limited resources.

This process is closely aligned with other processes in Portfolio Governance, providing communications with stakeholders when changes need to be made (see Figure 4-15).

Key activities include:

- Communicating portfolio decisions to key stakeholders, both for components included in and those excluded from the portfolio;

- Acquainting stakeholders with the communications plan which may include review cycles, timelines, etc.; and

- Communicating expected and actual portfolio results, identifying variances and corrective action.

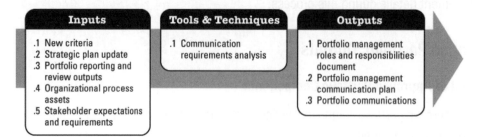

Figure 4-15. Communicate Portfolio Adjustment: Inputs, Tools & Techniques, and Outputs

4.7.1   Communicate Portfolio Adjustment: Inputs

.1 New Criteria

Described in Section 4.10.3.1.

.2 Strategic Plan Update

Updates to the strategic plan that resulted in the need to adjust the portfolio provide the impetus for communicating a portfolio change.

.3 Portfolio Reporting and Review Outputs

Described in Section 4.9.3.1 through 4.9.3.6.

.4 Organizational Process Assets

As issues arise, these should be addressed and resolved with the appropriate stakeholders. This includes relevant changes that occur throughout the management of the portfolio including strategic alignment, monitoring and controlling, and reallocation of organization process assets. Examples include:

- **Portfolio budget.** Communications about budget changes will assist organizational leaders in the realignment of a portfolio thus keeping portfolio return on investment (ROI) within the organizations vision and strategy.

- **Resources.** Changing organizational priorities that realign resource efforts, alter the work force, and/or modify the cost structure of resources will impact portfolio performance. The portfolio management team will need to determine if the resulting impact(s) are value-added or adverse to portfolio performance.

.5 Stakeholder Expectations and Requirements

Stakeholders for a portfolio come from a wide variety of areas and departments within an organization and are considered to be anyone whose interests will be affected, whether positively or negatively, by portfolio outcomes. It is important that an organization be aware of not only obvious stakeholders, such as senior leadership or the financial decision makers, but also considers those stakeholders specifically identified according to the goals and risk management strategies for the portfolio.

Section 2.2 lists portfolio stakeholders, including:

- Executive managers,

- Portfolio review board,

- Portfolio managers,

- Sponsors,

- Program managers,

- Project managers,

- Program/project management office, and

- Project team.

Additional stakeholders may exist within the organization or external to it. Stakeholders may also include individuals and groups who are not directly affected by the results of the program, but maintain an interest in the initiative.

4.7.2 Communicate Portfolio Adjustment: Tools and Techniques

.1 Communication Requirements Analysis

Analyzing communication requirements requires consideration of the needs of individual and groups of stakeholders; the type, format, and frequency of information they need; and the availability, cost to provide, and the value of that information.

Communication planning and execution should focus on the proactive and targeted development and delivery of key messages and engagement of key stakeholders at the right time and in the right manner. Communication of strategic changes to a portfolio must cross organizational and department boundaries to be truly successful in obtaining agreement. The traditional project boundaries of time, money, and scope must now fit into a strategic view of the portfolio's programs and projects.

Stakeholder management will drive the type of information communicated. All stakeholders, both internal and external, should be considered in a communications plan.

- Identify portfolio review points, for example:
  o Quarterly or biyearly review of portfolio,

- o Changes in organization policy or strategy, and

- o Sluggish portfolio movement as revealed through project reporting.

- Identify external stakeholders, for example:

  - o Suppliers of products required to support a project (such as servers, file units, etc.), and

  - o External resource providers (contractors, banks, insurance companies, etc.),

  - o Regulatory bodies (financial, professional, ethical, governmental, etc.), and

  - o Others (stockholders, stock analysts, etc.).

- Rank stakeholders according to the level of impact to portfolio success, for example:

  - o Organizational leadership and departmental managers,

  - o External suppliers,

  - o Internal resource managers and resources, and

  - o Financial stakeholders (budgets, procurement, HR, etc.).

- Determine type of communication in relation to the rank of stakeholders – for example:

  - o *Organizational leadership*—Anticipating and planning communications from the beginning;

  - o *Internal resource managers*—Communication exchange at a portfolio level during quarterly or biyearly portfolio reviews;

  - o *External suppliers*—When portfolio needs dictate change and this change shifts the organizational need to use a supplier, this stakeholder should be communicated with;

  - o *Financial stakeholders*—Communication timing for this group would depend on the type of stakeholder (budget might be quarterly while procurement might be monthly, for example); and

  - o *Project managers*—This would generally be the most frequent type of communication between a portfolio manager and a stakeholder often occurring weekly during staff meetings.

4.7.3 Communicate Portfolio Adjustment: Outputs

.1 Portfolio Management Roles and Responsibilities Document

Described in Section 4.8.2.1.

.2 Portfolio Management Communication Plan

The portfolio management communications plan defines all communication needs, establishes communication requirements, specifies frequency, and identifies recipients for information associated with the portfolio management process.

.3 Portfolio Communications

Reporting is a critical task for successful portfolio management. It provides stakeholders with a view on progress towards the achievement of the strategic vision and goals of the organization. It also informs organizational leadership if the portfolio is "doing the right work." Information is distributed to stakeholders to provide status on portfolio performance and to ensure that their expectations are being met.

4.8 Authorize Components

The purpose of this process is to formally allocate resources required to either develop business cases or execute selected components and to formally communicate portfolio-balancing decisions (see Figure 4-16).

Key activities include:

- Authorizing selected components, deactivating, and terminating components of the portfolio;

- Allocating resources to execute selected portfolio components;

- Reallocating budget and resources from deactivated and terminated components; and

- Communicating expected results (e.g., review cycles, timeline performance metrics, and required deliverables) for each selected component.

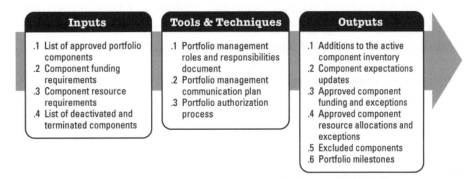

Figure 4-16. Authorize Components: Inputs, Tools & Techniques, and Outputs

4.8.1   Authorize Components: Inputs

.1 List of Approved Portfolio Components

This represents the complete list of components that have been approved for execution after developing a business case to confirm their feasibility or as planned (see 4.6.3.1).

.2 Component Funding Requirements

Funding requirement information is provided within either the component plan or business case.

.3 Component Resource Requirements

Resource requirement information is provided within either the component plan or business case.

.4 List of Deactivated and Terminated Components

The list represents those components that have been either deactivated or terminated in favor of pursuing higher priority and/or higher value components.

4.8.2 Authorize Components: Tools and Techniques

Tools and techniques for component authorization support communication of decisions about components included in the balanced portfolio. They also provide the means to assign roles, responsibilities, and performance milestones for implementation and monitoring. At this stage of the portfolio management process, available tools and techniques include, among others:

.1 Portfolio Management Roles and Responsibilities Document

The portfolio management roles and responsibilities document identifies stakeholders and then defines roles and specifies responsibilities for all participants in the portfolio management process.

.2 Portfolio Management Communication Plan

The portfolio management communication plan defines all communication needs, establishes communication requirements, specifies communication frequency, and identifies recipients for information associated with the portfolio management process.

.3 Portfolio Authorization Process

The authorization process specifies the formal authorization of the portfolio and its components, expectations, budgets, timing, and revisions.

4.8.3 Authorize Components: Outputs

.1 Additions to the Active Component Inventory

The list of all active components included in the portfolio. The list is updated with any changes related to new component authorizations.

.2 Component Expectations Updates

Any changes to the component expectations and required deliverables associated with the total set of components.

.3 Approved Component Funding and Exceptions

Component funding approvals or exceptions must be updated in response to changes in the set of active components.

.4 Approved Component Resource Allocations and Exceptions

Any changes to the component resource exceptions or approvals are described and the corresponding documents are updated and circulated according to a communications plan to key component stakeholders and other component support functions (e.g., finance).

.5 Excluded Components

Decisions to either remove components from the portfolio or exclude specific components within the portfolio are documented with the rationale for the decisions.

.6 Portfolio Milestones

The list of key deliverables and decision points for all components is consolidated to show the outcomes expected by the portfolio over time.

4.9 Review and Report Portfolio Performance

The purpose of this process is to gather performance indicators, report on them, and review the portfolio at an appropriate predetermined frequency to ensure both alignment with the organizational strategy and effective resource utilization (see Figure 4-17). Each component is reviewed individually to evaluate the individual performance contribution to the entire portfolio as well as a global review to see how the combination of investments is meeting the organization's needs.

The purpose of the review is to ensure that the portfolio contains only components that support achievement of the strategic goals. To achieve this, components must be added, reprioritized, or excluded based on their performance and ongoing alignment with the defined strategy in order to ensure effective management of the portfolio.

Activities in this process include:

- Reviewing component sponsorship, accountability, and other ownership criteria against organizational governance standards;

- Reviewing component priority, dependencies, scope, expected return, risks, and financial performance against portfolio control criteria and organizational perceived value and investment criteria;

- Reviewing expected impact of business forecasts, resource utilization, and capacity constraints on portfolio performance;

- Determining whether to continue with, add to, or terminate specific components or to reprioritize and realign them with strategic goals;

- Making recommendations and/or providing direction to component management; and

- Proposing changes to how the portfolio is managed (as needed).

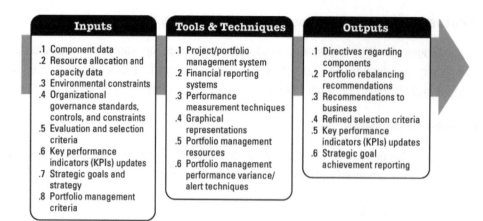

Figure 4-17. Review and Report Portfolio Performance: Inputs, Tools & Techniques, and Outputs

4.9.1 Review and Report Portfolio Performance: Inputs

.1 Component Data

Data related to each component are updated regularly during the life of the component and are provided to management for assessment. The information includes, but is not limited to, progress against plan, budget, expected return on investment, and priority.

.2 Resource Allocation and Capacity Data

Resources in this context include, for example, financial capacity, human resources, and production capacity. Capacity for all resource classes is examined so that managers can make prioritization and allocation decisions when selecting and evaluating components.

.3 Environmental Constraints

External constraints are imposed as either a directive or an influence beyond the control of the organization. Portfolio managers generally have no control over environmental constraints and have limited influence at best. Examples of environmental constraints include government regulations, interest rates, and seasonal weather.

.4 Organizational Governance Standards, Controls, and Constraints

Organizational governance standards are the organizational rules applied to managing portfolios and making decisions, such as human resource policies or the organization's strategy. Controls are checkpoints in the normal course of business, such as financial controls or the budgeting and allocation process. Constraints may include the organizational structure. Portfolio managers generally cannot control organizational constraints, but they may be able to exert influence upon them.

.5 Evaluation and Selection Criteria

Portfolio reviews use the evaluation and selection criteria to determine whether a particular component should remain part of the portfolio or be replaced by a component more likely to move the organization toward its goals.

.6 Key Performance Indicators (KPIs) Updates

The portfolio management team uses KPIs which are measures to determine whether a component is progressing as expected and whether the results are in line with what the organization expected.

.7 Strategic Goals and Strategy

Ultimately, the portfolio management team should align every component to the organization's strategic goals. Without such alignment, management should question why scarce resources are being allocated and why the component is being funded. Strategy is so fundamental to constructing the portfolio that any change in strategy will trigger an ad hoc review to ensure that all components continue to be aligned. When a major change occurs, such as an acquisition or market reorganization, the organization may also review its selection criteria and priorities along with the full set of components.

.8 Portfolio Management Criteria

These are specific objectives, constraints, and/or guidelines for use by the portfolio manager when managing the portfolio. Examples may include investment diversification objectives and risk tolerance thresholds.

4.9.2 Review and Report Portfolio Performance: Tools and Techniques

The portfolio management team should identify the performance report processes for monitoring and controlling that will provide value to each of the projects and programs being managed and ensure that portfolio review and performance reporting is accomplished successfully. The portfolio management team should identify the review and reporting tools and techniques that will provide measurable performance data.

The performance reporting tools and techniques should include but are not limited to:

.1 Project/Portfolio Management System

The portfolio management system is the central, typically electronic, repository for component-level information that can be rolled up for management analysis and decisions. It can exchange information with the systems and applications used by components.

.2 Financial Reporting Systems

Like the portfolio management system, the financial reporting systems provide data that managers use to determine whether components should be removed, reprioritized, or realigned within the portfolio.

.3 Performance Measurement Techniques

Each portfolio should specify performance measurement techniques that can be utilized via a reporting tool with defined and repeatable business rules.

The performance measurement techniques should include analytical and/or business rules that will support measurement of the project/program and its business case.

- **Progress measurement techniques.** The tools and techniques used at the portfolio level are similar to those used in a component, such as earned value.

- **Value measurement techniques.** The portfolio is also interested in the value resulting from the component's progress and how the component is contributing to the strategic goals. This is where management applies performance indicators and models which the organization may be using to measure strategic performance.

.4 Graphical Representations

Progress measurement techniques can also use graphical representations to help compare desired and/or planned situations with actual situations.

A typical graphical tool used is the "traffic light" analogy. Performance results are compared to planned/desired values for different indicators using a three-color coding representation with an identified scale acceptable by all and defined in the graph:

- **GREEN**—Evolution/forecast situation in line with desired results.

- **YELLOW**—Some difficulty encountered/perceived but effective corrective action possible or being implemented.

- **RED**—Critical situation calling for re-planning, an urgent intervention, that might even include postponing implementation or terminating the component.

"Radar" graphs can also be used to compare a project evolution with its desired performance and/or global portfolio performance criteria as illustrated in Figure 4-18.

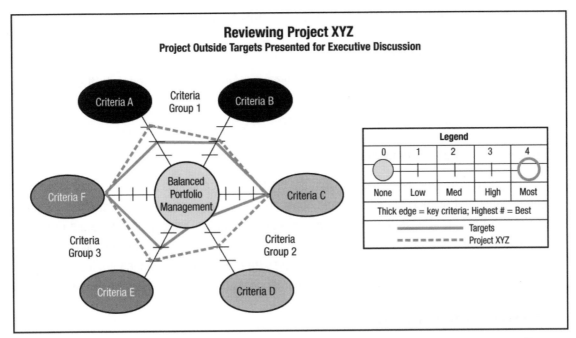

Figure 4-18. Graphical Representation of a Project and How It Performs Compared to Preset Performance Criteria

The same type of graphical tool can also be used to track the measures of several components as they change over time. Tracking may either refer to absolute values of the measures themselves or with reference to external benchmarks. Bubble graphs similar to Figures 4-13 and 4-14 can also be redrawn using new current components' performance results and other characteristics and compared to the results of the prior balancing step to see the evolution of the portfolio and its components over time and ensure that the desired overall balance and alignment are being maintained.

.5 Portfolio Management Resources

Depending upon the size and complexity of an organization, a single person or a team may manage the portfolio, and senior management or a specially chartered review board may make decisions regarding components. The portfolio manager should align performance review and reporting roles and responsibilities across each component.

.6 Portfolio Management Performance Variance/Alert Techniques

Performance variance/alert techniques should support content and be in a format that is standardized across each program and project within the portfolio.

4.9.3 Review and Report Portfolio Performance: Outputs

.1 Directives Regarding Components

Based on the review, the portfolio management team provides direction to the owners of the affected components. This may take the form of continuation, realignment of priorities or dependencies, resource reallocation, suspension, or termination.

.2 Portfolio Rebalancing Recommendations

The purpose of reviews is to ensure that the organization continues to invest in only those portfolio components that support stated strategic goals and objectives and to verify that those investments remain on-track to achieve these strategic goals and objectives. Periodically an output of the review process may be a recommendation to realign or discontinue funding of existing portfolio components or to establish new components in the portfolio. If and when the portfolio management team recommends that portfolio rebalancing may be necessary, component change process can be invoked.

.3 Recommendations to Business

Whereas directives to components flow downward in the organization, recommendations to business flow upward. Based on feedback from the components and insights gained from review, the portfolio management team may recognize new or altered dynamics that deserve attention from senior leadership. These recommendations may include changes to the strategic plan, to the component selection criteria, or to the portfolio review process itself.

.4 Refined Selection Criteria

Selection, evaluation, and prioritization criteria change as the organization evolves and the portfolio review process is where the effectiveness of these criteria is evaluated. The organization should refine the component criteria when needed to generate desired outcomes.

.5 Key Performance Indicators (KPIs) Updates

As with the component selection criteria, the organization must determine whether it is using the correct metrics and key performance indicators (KPIs) to make decisions. As appropriate, the portfolio management team must determine whether component results are being driven by the selected metrics and apply new or refined measurements when needed.

.6 Strategic Goal Achievement Reporting

The portfolio management team reports periodically or as needed on achievement of organizational goals and delivery of benefits to the organization by the portfolio.

4.10 Monitor Business Strategy Changes

The purpose of this process is to enable the portfolio management team to respond to changes in business strategy (see Figure 4-19). Incremental changes to the strategic plan generally do not require changes to the portfolio. However, significant changes in the business environment often result in a new strategic direction, thereby impacting the portfolio. A significant change in strategic direction will impact component categorization or prioritization and this will require rebalancing the portfolio.

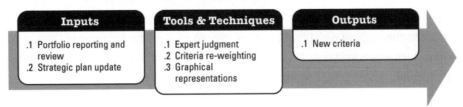

Figure 4-19. Monitor Business Strategy Changes: Inputs, Tools & Techniques, and Outputs

4.10.1 Monitor Business Strategy Changes: Inputs

.1 Portfolio Periodic Reporting and Review

Information about portfolio and component performance as well as recommendations to the organization is provided from portfolio periodic reporting and review.

.2 Strategic Plan Update

The organization's strategic plan should be the defining document and should be reflected in the program charter. The team should be familiar with the strategic plan and ensure that the portfolio and its components support the plan and that it is updated throughout the process.

4.10.2 Monitor Business Strategy Changes: Tools and Techniques

Tools and techniques for tracking and accounting for strategic changes aim at helping the organization to effectively take into account new business conditions arising over time. These should help measure the effect of these new conditions on the organization's current strategy, as well as to determine the appropriate responses to these changes. This might include putting into place new criteria/indicators and/or new criteria weights to re-evaluate the portfolio and realign and balance its current components or newly required components to respond to those strategic changes.

At this stage of the portfolio management process, available tools and techniques include, among others:

.1 Expert Judgment

Use expert judgment often to assess whether a strategic change will occur and its likely effect on the current portfolio.

.2 Criteria Re-weighting

Changing business conditions might necessitate reconsideration of the original criteria used for both aligning and monitoring the project portfolio and its components. This will result in a change in the weights assigned to key indicators and criteria and/or inclusion of new criteria for the subsequent realignment of the components to address new business conditions.

.3 Graphical Representations

The portfolio management team can use graphical representations to illustrate required changes to portfolio management criteria following a change in business conditions. The example illustrated in Figure 4-20 shows that strategic changes, shown as dark ovals at Criteria A and Criteria B, call for changes to the original weighting to occur, shown as dark circles against Criteria A and Criteria E, due to new business conditions. This causes re-weighting of two of the six criteria used for portfolio management by the impacted organization.

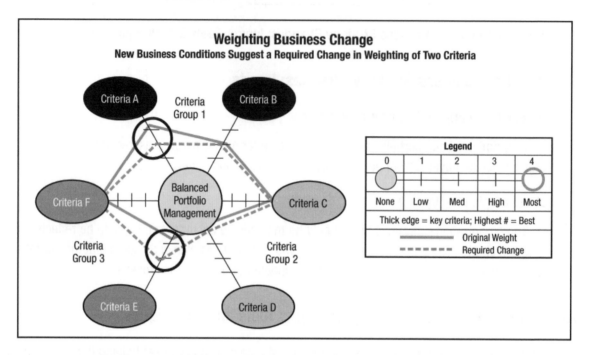

Figure 4-20. Graphical Representation of a Required Change in the Weighting to Use for Two Criteria

4.10.3 Monitor Business Strategy Changes: Outputs

.1 New Criteria

As environments inside and outside the organization change, criteria for determining the composition and direction of the portfolio may also change. New leadership may want to adjust business strategies according to different goals. Market maturation or sector focus change may require different financial profit thresholds. When the need for new criteria becomes evident, the portfolio management team needs to examine the current criteria in the strategic plan and move ahead with appropriate changes, usually focusing first on categorization (see Section 4.2). If strategic change is not occurring, then efforts should focus on portfolio balancing (see Section and 4.6).

CHAPTER 5

PORTFOLIO RISK MANAGEMENT

Portfolio risk is an uncertain event, set of events, or conditions that if they occur, have one or more effects, either positive or negative, on at least one strategic business objective of the portfolio. A risk may have one or more causes and, if it occurs, the corresponding effects have an impact on one or more portfolio success criteria. An example of an internal cause would be a limit on the number of design personnel available; an external cause would be the passage of legislation which mandates immediate additional project work. The corresponding risks are:

- The design personnel available and assigned may not be adequate for the full mix of activities, with a negative impact on performance; and

- Compliance with new legislation may require the postponement of active or planned projects, thereby delaying or reducing the corresponding benefits.

Risk conditions could include aspects of an organization's environment that may contribute to portfolio risk, such as poor management practices (a negative risk), integrated management systems (positive), an excessive number of concurrent projects (negative), or dependency on external participants who are highly specialized (positive).

The objectives of Portfolio Risk Management are to increase the probability and impact of positive events and to decrease the probability and impact of events adverse to the portfolio. Portfolio Risk Management includes the processes concerned with conducting risk identification, analysis, response development, as well as monitoring and control of the risks. These processes are carried out as an integral part of the overall portfolio management life cycle.

There are four Portfolio Risk Management processes:

1. **Identify Portfolio Risks**—Determining which risks might affect the portfolio and documenting their characteristics (see Section 5.1).

2. **Analyze Portfolio Risks**—Assessing and combining the probability of occurrence and impact of identified risks; numerically analyzing the overall effect of selected risks on the portfolio; prioritizing risks for subsequent further analysis or action (see Section 5.2).

3. **Develop Portfolio Risk Responses**—Developing options and actions to enhance opportunities and to reduce threats to portfolio objectives (see Section 5.3).

4. **Monitor and Control Portfolio Risks**—Tracking identified risks, monitoring residual risks, identifying new risks, executing risk response plans, and evaluating their effectiveness throughout the portfolio life cycle (see Section 5.4).

These processes interact with each other and with the processes in the other portfolio management Knowledge Areas. Each process involves effort from one or more persons or groups of persons based on the needs of the portfolio and its components. Although the processes are presented here as discrete elements with well-defined interfaces, in practice they may overlap and interact in ways not detailed here. Figure 5-1 provides a list of the inputs, tools and techniques, and outputs of the portfolio risk management processes and Figure 5-2 provides a flow diagram.

Figure 5-1. Portfolio Risk Management Overview

Portfolio risk has its origins in the uncertainty that is present in all endeavors. Known risks are those that have been identified and analyzed. It may be possible to plan for known risks using the processes described in this chapter. Unknown risks cannot be managed proactively, and a prudent response by the portfolio management team may be to allocate general contingency against such risks, as well as against any known risks for which it may not be cost effective or possible to develop a specific proactive response.

Organizations perceive risks as threats to strategic success or as opportunities to enhance chances or level of success. Risks that are threats to the portfolio objectives may be accepted if the risk is in balance with the reward that may be gained by taking the risk. For example, delaying a project so that all of the key resources can work on another component of the portfolio may help achieve an earlier completion date for that component and realize the corresponding benefits earlier.

Persons and, by extension, organizations have attitudes toward risk that affect both the accuracy of their perception of risk and the way they respond. Attitudes about risk should be made explicit and translated into measurable criteria wherever possible. A consistent approach to risk that meets the organization's requirements should be developed for the entire portfolio and applied to the corresponding components. Risk responses reflect an organization's stated balance between risk acceptance and risk avoidance. Communication about risk and its responses should be open and honest.

One key success factor to portfolio management is the development of a balanced portfolio which takes into consideration the level of risk tolerance of the organization. When balancing the portfolio, the portfolio management team must take into account the risks inherent in the final set of components to be included in the portfolio, the corresponding risk responses, and their potential effect on tactical and strategic objectives, such as time, cost, and return on portfolio assets.

Another key success factor for portfolio management is organizational commitment to the proactive and consistent management of risk.

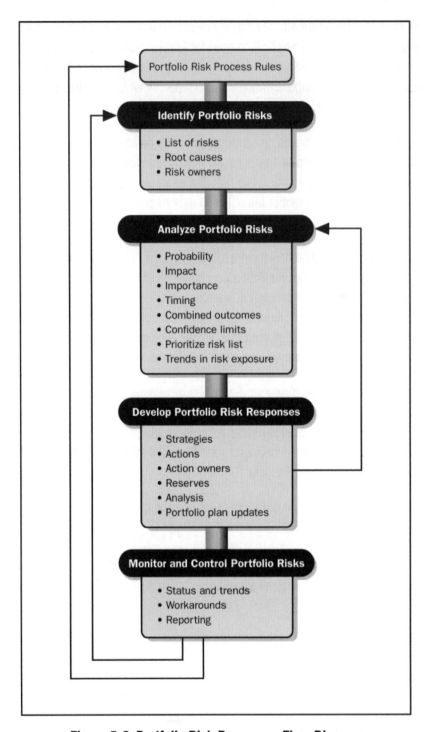

Figure 5-2. Portfolio Risk Processes Flow Diagram

Portfolio balancing implies the use of progressive elaboration of the balanced portfolio as shown in Figure 5-3: outputs from Analyze Portfolio Risks are inputs for balancing. In order to provide progressive elaboration of the balanced portfolio, Develop Risk Responses may need to be followed by an additional iteration of the Identify Portfolio Risks and Analyze Portfolio Risks processes to determine response interactions and overall impact before a balanced content can be confirmed.

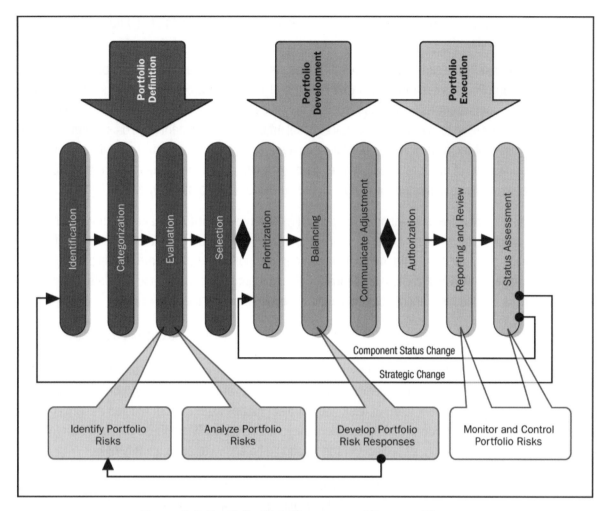

Figure 5-3. Portfolio Risk Management Process Diagram

5.1 Identify Portfolio Risks

The Risk Identification Process reveals risks that might affect the portfolio and documents their characteristics (see Figure 5-4). A portfolio comprises the following different categories of risks:

- **Structural risks.** These are the risks associated with the way in which the portfolio is composed, and the potential interactions among the components. One obvious category of threats in this area is associated with resource availability. Features of the portfolio structure can be root causes of a number of risks.

- **Component risks.** These are the risks from the individual components that have been escalated from the component managers for information or action at the portfolio level. Component risks are generally associated with one or more of the triple-constraint parameters of the component deliverables (time, cost, or scope.) The portfolio manager needs to evaluate the corresponding effect of the risks on the success criteria of the portfolio since the portfolio success criteria will normally be at the strategic level. While a portfolio may contain one or more programs and these may also contain programs or projects, the portfolio manager may need to consider component risks at each of these levels.

- **Overall risks.** In the same way that overall project risks are more than just the sum of individual project risks, portfolio risks are more than just the sum of the portfolio component risks. The interactions between component risks can lead to the emergence of one or more overall risks. A special set of tools may be used to evaluate the overall effect of interlinked component risks on strategic objectives. The quality of the organization's portfolio management is also a factor for overall risk: governance and application of best practices can provide opportunities for improvement whereas overambitious plans, as well as inconsistent or rapidly changing strategy can present threats to success.

In order to ensure effective separation of responsibilities between portfolio managers and the managers of component programs or projects, portfolio managers should focus their attention on these portfolio-level risks. The portfolio manager should not become involved in component risks that are the responsibility of the component manager; however, a component manager should identify, document, and escalate to the portfolio manager any risks beyond his authority or which seem likely to affect portfolio objectives.

The portfolio manager needs to define all the above aspects in a portfolio risk management plan.

Participants in risk identification activities can include the following: business managers, managers of any portfolio, program or project management offices concerned, project managers, portfolio management team members, risk management team (if assigned), subject matter experts from outside the project teams, customers, end users, stakeholders, and other risk management experts. While these personnel are often key participants for risk identification, all project personnel should be encouraged to identify risks.

Identify Portfolio Risks is an iterative process because new risks may surface over time. The frequency and participants of each iteration may vary. The portfolio management team should be involved in the process so that they can develop and maintain a sense of ownership of, and responsibility for, the risks and associated risk response actions. Stakeholders outside the portfolio management team may provide additional information.

The Identify Portfolio Risks process usually leads to the Analyze Portfolio Risks process (Section 5.2). On some occasions, as risks are identified, suggestions regarding their response may be obtained. These suggested responses should be recorded for further analysis and implementation in the Develop Portfolio Risk Responses process (Section 5.3).

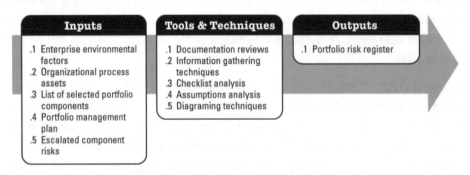

Inputs	Tools & Techniques	Outputs
.1 Enterprise environmental factors .2 Organizational process assets .3 List of selected portfolio components .4 Portfolio management plan .5 Escalated component risks	.1 Documentation reviews .2 Information gathering techniques .3 Checklist analysis .4 Assumptions analysis .5 Diagraming techniques	.1 Portfolio risk register

Figure 5-4. Identify Portfolio Risks: Inputs, Tools & Techniques, and Outputs

5.1.1   Identify Portfolio Risks: Inputs

.1   Enterprise Environmental Factors

Published information, including commercial databases, academic studies, benchmarking, or other industry studies, may also be useful in identifying risks (Section 2.3.4).

.2   Organizational Process Assets

Information on prior projects may be available from historic files, including actual data and lessons learned (Section 4.7.1.4).

.3   List of Selected Portfolio Components

The list of selected components becomes the baseline against which risk is assessed.

.4   Portfolio Management Plan

The Identify Portfolio Risks process also requires an understanding of the schedule, risk, cost, and quality management plans found in the portfolio management plan. Key inputs from the risk management plan to the Risk Identification process are the assignments of roles and responsibilities, provision for risk management activities in the budget and schedule, and categories of risk (5.1.1.5), which are sometimes expressed in a risk breakdown structure (RBS) (see Figure 5-3). Outputs of other Knowledge Area processes such as Portfolio Governance should be reviewed to identify possible risks across the entire portfolio.

.5   Escalated Component Risks

The portfolio components contain two categories of risk:

- Those which are likely to affect the portfolio significantly. The component manager needs to escalate these to the portfolio manager for consideration and potential action.

- Those within the scope and authority levels defined for the component and that the component manager can deal with without impacting or needing assistance from, portfolio management.

The portfolio manager needs to state the level of the component manager's authority (e.g., maximum allowed schedule slip in a project) in the corresponding chartering document in order to define the thresholds at which escalation should be carried out for information and for action at the portfolio level.

5.1.2   Identify Portfolio Risks: Tools and Techniques

.1   Documentation Reviews

A structured review may be performed of component documentation, including plans, assumptions, files from prior projects, and other information. Risks can be identified not only from the content of the individual documents but also from the level of alignment between those plans and the portfolio requirements and assumptions.

.2 Information Gathering Techniques

Examples of information gathering techniques used in identifying risk can include:

- **Brainstorming.** The goal of brainstorming is to obtain a comprehensive list of risks. The portfolio management team often performs brainstorming with a multidisciplinary set of experts not on the team. The group generates ideas about portfolio and component risks under the leadership of a facilitator. Categories of risk as detailed in a risk breakdown structure (RBS) (Figure 5-5) can be used as a framework. The group then assigns categories and refines definitions for identified risks.

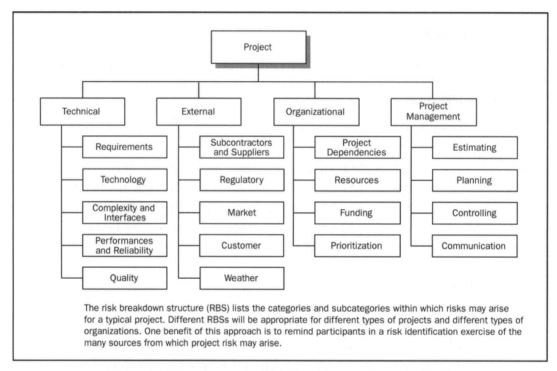

The risk breakdown structure (RBS) lists the categories and subcategories within which risks may arise for a typical project. Different RBSs will be appropriate for different types of projects and different types of organizations. One benefit of this approach is to remind participants in a risk identification exercise of the many sources from which project risk may arise.

Figure 5-5. Examples of a Risk Breakdown Structure (RBS)

- **Delphi technique.** The Delphi technique is a way to reach a consensus within a group of experts. Risk experts participate in this technique anonymously. A facilitator uses a questionnaire to solicit ideas about the important portfolio risks. The facilitator summarizes the responses and then redistributes them to the experts for further comment. Consensus may be reached in a few rounds of this process. The Delphi technique helps minimize the occurrence of bias in the data and ensures that each participant's input is taken into account objectively.

- **Interviewing.** Interviewing experienced component participants, stakeholders, and subject matter experts can help identify risks. Interviews are one of the main sources of risk identification data gathering.

- **Root cause identification.** This is an inquiry into the essential causes of a risk or set of risks. It can help to enhance the definition of the risk and allows grouping risks by causes. Effective risk responses can be developed if the root cause of the risk is addressed.

- **Strengths, weaknesses, opportunities, and threats (SWOT) analysis.** This technique ensures examination of the portfolio from each of the SWOT perspectives to increase the breadth of considered risks.

.3 Checklist Analysis

Risk identification checklists can be developed based on historical information and knowledge that has been accumulated from previous projects and from other sources of information. The lowest level of the RBS can also be used as a risk checklist. While a checklist can be quick and simple, it is impossible to build an exhaustive one. Care should be taken to explore items that do not explicitly appear on the checklist. The checklist should be reviewed during component closure to improve it for use on other components within the portfolio.

.4 Assumptions Analysis

The portfolio management team conceives and develops every portfolio based on a set of hypotheses, scenarios, or assumptions. Assumptions analysis is a tool that explores the validity of assumptions as they apply to the portfolio and its components. It identifies risks due to inaccuracy, inconsistency, or incompleteness of assumptions. In a similar manner, the portfolio management team may identify additional risks by considering the possibility of relaxing one or more portfolio constraints.

.5 Diagramming Techniques

Risk diagramming techniques may include the following:

- **Cause-and-effect diagrams.** These are also known as Ishikawa or fishbone diagrams, and are useful for identifying causes of risks (Figure 5-6).

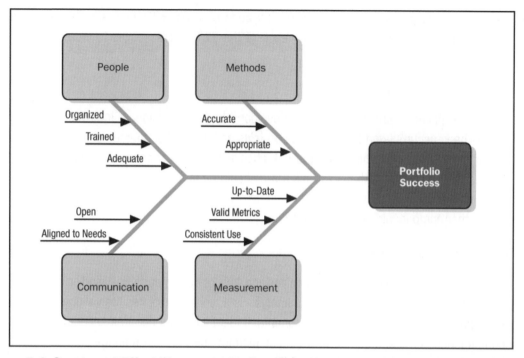

Figure 5-6. Cause-and-Effect Diagram to Analyze Potential Contributions to Portfolio Success

- **System or process flow charts.** These are charts that are used to describe the sequence and relationships of various elements of a system or process, such as Figure 5-2.

- **Influence diagrams.** These are graphical representations of situations showing causal influences, chronological ordering of events, and other relationships among variables and outcomes (Figure 5-7).

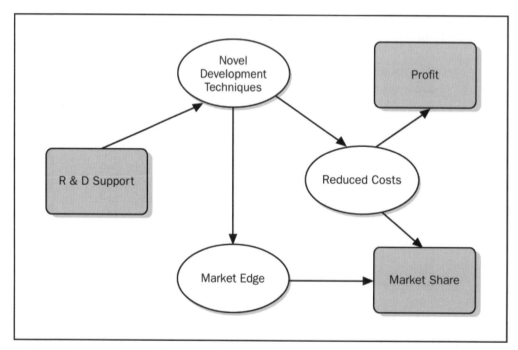

Figure 5-7. Influence Diagram Applied to Selection of a Category of Investment

- **Risk-component chart.** The grouping of risks by category and by component can benefit from a pictorial output (Figure 5-8).

- **Others.** The portfolio management team may use additional tools, such as system dynamics, causal maps, and force-field analysis.

Risk ID	Component 1			Component 2			Component 3			Etc.		
	S	C	O	S	C	O	S	C	O	S	C	O
	Structural Risks											
R1	★			★			★					
	Component Risks											
R2		★										
R3		★										
R4		★		★								
R5								★				
	Overall Risks											
R6			★	★								
R7			★					★				
Etc.												

Note: Structural Risk R1 affects three components (Component 1, Component 2, and Component 3); Risk R4 appears in two components (Component 1 and Component 2), which suggests that there may be a common cause; Risk R6 arises from the combined effect from Components 1 and 2.

Figure 5-8. Risk Component Chart

5.1.3 Identify Portfolio Risks: Outputs

.1 Portfolio Risk Register

The primary outputs from Risk Identification are the initial entries into the risk register, which becomes a component of the portfolio management plan. The development of the risk register begins with the Identify Portfolio Risk process. The risk register ultimately contains the outcomes of the other risk management processes. Initially it contains the following information:

- **List of identified risks.** The identified risks, including their root causes and uncertain assumptions, are described. For example, one component project may finish late and consequently fail to free up resources that were expected to be available to work on another component which in turn potentially invalidates the justification for undertaking this later component. A competitor may release a product that affects some of the strategic goals of the portfolio thereby enhancing the justification for some of the active or future components.

- **Risk Owner.** The portfolio manager designates a person accountable for effective management of the corresponding risk. This person's role is to ensure analysis and, as necessary, to assign response-related actions, and to monitor the situation for as long as the risk is current.

- **List of potential responses.** Potential responses to a risk may be identified during the Risk Identification process. These responses, if identified, may be useful as inputs to the Develop Portfolio Risk Response process (Section 5.3).

- **Root causes of risk.** These are the fundamental conditions or events that may give rise to the identified risk.

- **Updated risk categories.** The process of identifying risks can lead to new risk categories being added. The risk breakdown structure (RBS) in the portfolio management plan may have to be enhanced or amended based on the outcomes of the Identify Portfolio Risk process.

The information in the risk register will subsequently be used and updated by other portfolio management and portfolio risk management processes.

5.2 Analyze Portfolio Risks

Portfolio risk analysis includes methods for prioritizing the identified risks for further action (see Figure 5-9). Organizations can improve a portfolio's performance most effectively by focusing on high-priority risks. The Analyze Portfolio Risks process determines the priority of identified risks using their probability of occurrence and the corresponding impact on portfolio objectives, for example, business enhancement, return on investment, as well as other factors. The analysis also takes into account the risk tolerance of the organization and the individual stakeholders.

Definitions of the levels of probability and impact as well as expert interviewing, can help to correct biases that are often present in the data used in this process. The time criticality of risk-related actions may magnify the perceived magnitude of a risk. Evaluating the quality of the available information on component risks also helps understand the assessment of the risk's importance to the portfolio.

The portfolio manager should ensure that the Analyze Portfolio Risks process is repeated periodically during the portfolio's life cycle to stay current with changes in the portfolio's risks.

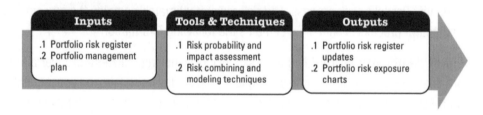

Inputs	Tools & Techniques	Outputs
.1 Portfolio risk register	.1 Risk probability and impact assessment	.1 Portfolio risk register updates
.2 Portfolio management plan	.2 Risk combining and modeling techniques	.2 Portfolio risk exposure charts

Figure 5-9. Analyze Portfolio Risks: Inputs, Tools & Techniques, and Outputs

5.2.1 Analyze Portfolio Risks: Inputs

.1 Portfolio Risk Register

Described in 5.1.3.1. This provides the list of identified risks plus any additional information from previous iterations of the risk management processes.

.2 Portfolio Management Plan

One important component of the portfolio management plan is the risk management plan. It defines roles and responsibilities for conducting risk management, budgets, schedule activities for risk management, risk categories, definition of probability and impact, the probability and impact matrix, and revised stakeholders' risk tolerances (also see organization environmental factors in Section 5.1.1.1). If any of this information is not already available, the team responsible for portfolio risk management needs to develop it as part of this analysis process.

5.2.2 Analyze Portfolio Risks: Tools and Techniques

.1 Risk Probability and Impact Assessment

Risk probability assessment determines the likelihood of occurrence of each specific risk. Risk impact assessment investigates the potential effect, both negative effects for threats and positive effects for opportunities, on one or more of the portfolio's objectives.

Probability and impact are assessed for each identified risk. Risks can be assessed in interviews or meetings with participants who have been selected for their familiarity with the risk categories on the agenda. Portfolio management team members and knowledgeable persons from outside the portfolio are included. Expert judgment is required since there may be little information on risks from the organization's database of past portfolios, programs, and projects. An experienced facilitator may be required to lead the discussion since the participants may have little experience with risk assessment.

The level of probability for each risk and its impact on each objective is evaluated during the interview or meeting. Explanatory details, including assumptions justifying the levels assigned, are also recorded. Risk probabilities and impacts are rated according to the definitions given in the risk management plan. Sometimes, risks with obviously low ratings of probability and impact will not be retained for additional work, but will be included in a general category for monitoring (a "watchlist").

Typical tools are:

- Interviewing techniques,

- Probability distributions,

- Probability and impact matrix as shown in Figure 5-10, and

- Financial analysis tools (expected monetary value, economic value added, etc.) as shown in Figure 5-11.

Probability and Impact Matrix

Probability	Threats					Opportunities				
0.90	0.05	0.09	0.18	0.36	0.72	0.72	0.36	0.18	0.09	0.05
0.70	0.04	0.07	0.14	0.28	0.56	0.56	0.28	0.14	0.07	0.04
0.50	0.03	0.05	0.10	0.20	0.40	0.40	0.20	0.10	0.05	0.03
0.30	0.02	0.03	0.06	0.12	0.24	0.24	0.12	0.06	0.03	0.02
0.10	0.01	0.01	0.02	0.04	0.08	0.08	0.04	0.02	0.01	0.01
	0.05	0.10	0.20	0.40	0.80	0.80	0.40	0.20	0.10	0.05

Impact (ratio scale) on an objective (e.g., cost, time, scope or quality)

■ = High   □ = Moderate   ■ = Low

Note: Each risk is rated on its probability of occurring and impact on an objective if it does occur. The organization's thresholds for low, moderate or high risks are shown in the matrix and determine whether the risk is scored as high, moderate or low for that objective.

Figure 5-10. Probability and Impact Matrix

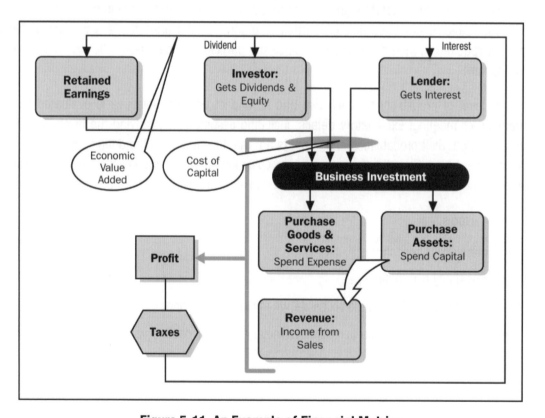

Figure 5-11. An Example of Financial Metrics

.2 Risk Combining and Modeling Techniques

As described in 5.1 (Identify Portfolio Risks), portfolio risk is the result of the risks generated by the components as well as those due to the structure and composition of the portfolio. The interaction and combined effects of these risks also need to be evaluated in order to understand the total set of portfolio-level risks. Typical tools are as follows:

- **Sensitivity analysis.** Sensitivity analysis helps determine which risks have the most potential impact on the portfolio. It examines the extent to which the uncertainty of each element affects the respective objective when all other uncertain elements are held at their baseline values. One typical graphical output of sensitivity analysis is the tornado diagram; this is useful for displaying which parameters lead to a high degree of variability and which have less effect.

- **Modeling and simulation**. Simulation uses a model that translates the uncertainties specified at a detailed level of the portfolio into their potential combined impact on portfolio objectives. Simulations are typically performed using the Monte Carlo technique. In a simulation, the model is computed many times (iterated). At each iteration, the input values (such as cost of project elements or duration of schedule activities) are randomized in accordance with the probability distribution of the corresponding variable. The outputs of each iteration are consolidated to provide a frequency distribution for the values of each key parameter (such as total cost or completion date) (Figure 5-12).

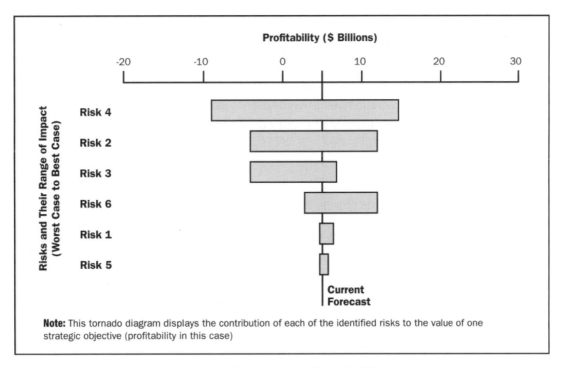

Figure 5-12. Example of a Tornado Diagram

5.2.3 Analyze Portfolio Risks: Outputs

.1 Portfolio Risk Register Updates

The portfolio manager updates the portfolio risk register which is included in the portfolio management plan. The portfolio risk register updates from the Analyze Portfolio Risks process include:

- **Relative ranking or priority list of portfolio risks.** The probability and impact matrix can be used to classify risks according to their individual significance. The portfolio manager can then use the prioritized list to focus attention on those items of high significance to the portfolio. This ranking can be carried out separately for each portfolio success criterion to take into account the different importance the organization may have placed on the various objectives. The portfolio manager should include a description of the basis for the assigned probability and the impact for risks assessed as important to the portfolio.

- **Risks grouped by categories.** Risk categorization can reveal common root causes of risk or portfolio areas requiring particular attention. Discovering concentrations of risk may improve the effectiveness of risk response planning.

- **List of risks requiring response in the near term.** The portfolio manager may put into different groups those risks that require an urgent response and those that can be handled at a later date.

- **Watchlists of low-priority risks.** The portfolio manager can place on a list for continued monitoring risks that are not assessed as significant.

- **Trends in risk analysis results.** As the analysis is repeated, trends for particular risks may become apparent. This information may be used to assess the effectiveness of earlier responses, and to decide whether to modify the urgency of any risk responses or other risk management actions.

.2 Portfolio Risk Exposure Charts

Portfolio risk exposure charts provide the following information:

- **Outcome probability analysis of the portfolio.** The portfolio manager makes estimates of potential portfolio outcomes with respect to the success criteria listing the possible values of the corresponding performance indicators with their associated confidence levels. This output is typically expressed as a cumulative distribution (Figure 5-13) that the project manager can use to set realistic targets in line with stakeholder risk tolerances.

- **Probability of achieving portfolio objectives.** The portfolio manager can estimate the probability of achieving specific objectives under the current plan using modeling techniques as explained above.

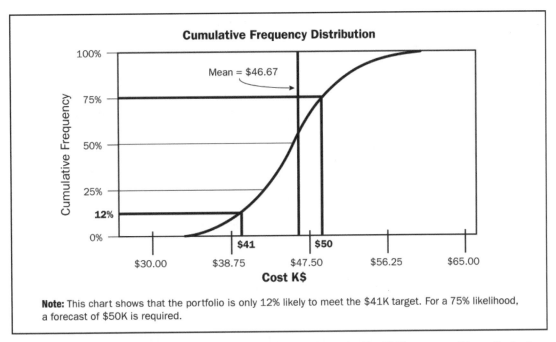

Figure 5-13. Cumulative Cost Chart for the Spend on the Portfolio over a Given Period

5.3 Develop Portfolio Risk Responses

Risk response development is the process of developing options and determining actions to enhance opportunities and reduce threats to the portfolio's objectives (see Figure 5-14). It needs to take into account all of the risks that were assessed as significant in the Analyze Portfolio Risks process. Develop Portfolio Risk Responses addresses the risks by their priority and incorporates the corresponding resources and activities into the budget, schedule, and portfolio management plan. The risk owner is responsible for selecting the best risk response when several options are available. The portfolio manager, in agreement with the risk owner, will assign one person to take responsibility for each agreed-upon risk response (the "portfolio risk response owner").

Planned risk responses must be appropriate to the significance of the risk, cost effective in meeting the challenge, timely, realistic within the context of the portfolio, agreed upon by all parties involved, and owned by an accountable person.

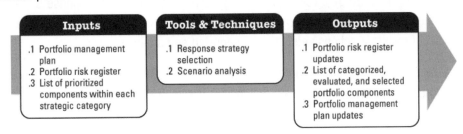

Figure 5-14. Develop Portfolio Risk Responses: Inputs, Tools &Techniques, and Outputs

5.3.1 Develop Portfolio Risk Responses: Inputs

Important inputs to Develop Portfolio Risk Responses include the relative rating or priority listing of portfolio risks, a list of risks requiring response in the near term, a list of risks requiring additional analysis and response, trends in risk analysis results, root causes, risks grouped by categories, lists of potential responses, risk owners, symptoms, and warning signs, and a watchlist of low-priority risks.

.1 Portfolio Management Plan

Within the portfolio management plan, important components of the risk management plan include risk thresholds (for low, moderate, and high risks), roles and responsibilities, guidelines on use of tools, and details of the time and budget allocated to portfolio risk management.

.2 Portfolio Risk Register

The risk register is first developed in the Identify Portfolio Risks process and is updated during the Analyze Portfolio Risks process.

.3 List of Prioritized Components within Each Strategic Category

This list is the prioritized list of components for portfolio balancing along with appropriate documentation.

5.3.2 Develop Portfolio Risk Responses: Tools and Techniques

Several risk response strategies can be considered for each risk. The portfolio manager along with the risk owner should select the strategy or mix of strategies most likely to be effective. The risk owner must make decisions to choose the most appropriate response strategy or mix of strategies and then develop specific actions to implement that decision. The risk owner may select primary and alternate strategies. The risk owner can develop contingency plans and identify the conditions that trigger their execution. Often a contingency reserve is allocated for time or cost. Finally, the risk owner can develop a fallback plan for execution if the selected strategy turns out not to be sufficiently effective.

.1 Response Strategy Selection

Selection of the strategy involves examining each of the potential response strategies and then selecting the most appropriate approach. This needs to be carried out for threats and for opportunities, and the set of resultant actions needs to be integrated and analyzed.

- **Strategies for Threats.** Three strategies typically deal with risks that may have negative impacts on portfolio objectives if they occur. These strategies are to avoid, transfer, or mitigate the risk:

  o *Avoid.* Risk avoidance involves changing the portfolio management plan to eliminate the threat posed by an adverse risk, to isolate the portfolio's objectives from the risk's impact, or to relax or abandon the objective that is in jeopardy.

---

  o *Transfer.* Risk transference requires shifting the negative impact of a threat with, potentially, ownership of the response, to a third party. Transferring the risk simply gives another party responsibility for its management; it does not eliminate it. Transferring liability for risk is most effective in dealing with financial risk exposure. Risk transference nearly always involves payment of a risk premium to the party taking on the risk. Transference tools can be quite diverse and include, but are not limited to, the use of insurance, performance bonds, warranties, guarantees, etc. The portfolio manager may use contracts to transfer liability for specified risks to another party.

  o *Mitigate.* Risk mitigation implies a reduction in the probability and/or impact of an adverse risk event to an acceptable threshold. Taking early action to reduce the probability and/or impact of a risk occurring is often more effective than trying to repair the damage after the risk has occurred.

- **Strategies for Opportunities.** Three responses are suggested to deal with risks with potentially positive impacts on portfolio objectives. These strategies are to exploit, share, or enhance the risk.

  o *Exploit.* This strategy may be selected for risks with positive impacts where the organization wishes to ensure that the opportunity is realized. This strategy seeks to eliminate the uncertainty associated with a particular upside risk by making the opportunity definitely happen. Examples of such responses would be: assigning more talented resources to a component to reduce the time to completion, or expanding the scope of a deliverable to address a broader market.

  o *Share.* Sharing a positive risk involves allocating some or all of the ownership to a third party more likely to be able to exploit the opportunity, in exchange for a participation in the corresponding benefits. Examples of sharing actions include forming risk-sharing partnerships, teams, special-purpose companies, or joint ventures, with the express purpose of managing opportunities.

  o *Enhance.* This strategy modifies the "size" of an opportunity by increasing probability and/or positive impact and by identifying and maximizing key drivers of these positive-impact risks. Seeking to facilitate or strengthen the cause of the opportunity and proactively targeting and reinforcing its trigger conditions might increase probability. Impact drivers can also be targeted, seeking to increase the component's susceptibility to the opportunity.

- **Strategies for Both Threats and Opportunities:**

  o *Acceptance.* Some risks have to be accepted because it is not possible to respond to all of the risks in a portfolio and remain viable. Acceptance indicates that the portfolio management team has decided not to change the portfolio management plan to deal with a risk or is unable to identify any other suitable response strategy. It may be adopted for either threats or opportunities. Acceptance can be either passive or active. Passive acceptance requires no action leaving the portfolio management team to deal with the threats or opportunities as they occur. The most common active acceptance strategy is to establish a contingency reserve, including amounts of time, money, or resources to handle known—or even sometimes potential, unknown—threats or opportunities.

○ *Contingent Response Strategy.* The portfolio manager designs some responses for use only if certain events occur. For some risks, it is appropriate for the portfolio management team to make a response plan that will only be executed under certain predefined conditions, if it is believed that there will be sufficient warning to implement the plan. The portfolio manager should define and track events or conditions that trigger the contingency response, such as missing intermediate milestones or gaining higher priority with a supplier.

.2 Scenario Analysis

Once the set of actions based on the selected strategies has been defined, the potential result of these actions must be assessed with respect to the success criteria of the portfolio. This may entail repeating the processes for identifying and analyzing portfolio risks. It also entails modifying the existing plans where necessary in order to ensure that the response actions become an integral part of the portfolio plan.

5.3.3 Develop Portfolio Risk Responses: Outputs

.1 Portfolio Risk Register Updates

The portfolio manager develops the risk register in the Identify Portfolio Risks process, and updates it during Analyze Portfolio Risks process. In the Develop Portfolio Risk Responses process, appropriate responses are chosen, agreed-upon, included in the risk register, and integrated into the portfolio management plan. The risk register should be written to a level of detail that corresponds with the priority ranking and the planned response. Often the high and moderate risks are addressed in detail. Risks judged to be of low priority are included in a watchlist for periodic monitoring. Components of the risk register at this point can include:

- Identified risks, their descriptions, their causes, area(s) of the portfolio (component, etc.) affected, and how they may affect portfolio objectives;

- Risk owners and assigned responsibilities;

- Outputs from the Analyze Portfolio Risks process, including prioritized lists of portfolio risks and probabilistic analysis;

- Agreed-upon response strategies;

- Specific actions to implement the chosen response strategy along with the identification of the designated risk response owner;

- Symptoms and warning signs of the risk occurrence;

- Budget and schedule components required for implementing the chosen responses;

- Contingency reserves of time and cost designed to provide for stakeholders' risk tolerances;

- Contingency plans and triggers for their execution;

- Fallback plans for use when the primary response to a risk that has occurred proves to be inadequate;

- Secondary risks that arise as a direct outcome of implementing a risk response, along with the selected response strategies and plans for them; and

- Residual risks that are expected to remain after planned responses have been taken, as well as those that have been deliberately accepted.

.2 List of Categorized, Evaluated, and Selected Portfolio Components

The set of portfolio components may be affected by the modification, addition, or removal of components in line with the selected risk response actions. The portfolio may require re-balancing in order to accommodate these changes, as shown in Figure 5-3.

.3 Portfolio Management Plan Updates

Risk response plans, once agreed upon, must be fed back into the appropriate processes in other Knowledge Areas, for example through updates to the portfolio's budget to cover preventive actions or to allow for contingency reserves, schedule, and resource assignments. To ensure that agreed-upon actions are implemented and monitored as part of ongoing portfolio management, the portfolio management plan is updated as response activities are formally approved.

5.4 Monitor and Control Portfolio Risks

Once the planned risk responses have been included in the portfolio management plan, the portfolio management team executes them just like any other approved portfolio activity. Monitor and Control Portfolio Risks aims to ensure effective control of portfolio uncertainty during portfolio execution (see Figure 5-15). It includes the following:

- Keeping track of the identified risks including those on the watchlist;

- Monitoring trigger conditions and, as necessary, invoking the corresponding contingency plans;

- Monitoring residual risks;

- Reanalyzing existing risks;

- Tracking changes in the stakeholder community;

- Reviewing the execution of risk responses while simultaneously evaluating their effectiveness; and

- Identifying, analyzing, and planning for newly arising risks.

The Monitor and Control Portfolio Risks process applies techniques, such as variance and trend analysis, which require the use of performance data generated during component execution. Along with the other risk management processes, it is an ongoing process throughout the entire portfolio life cycle. Other purposes of the Monitor and Control Portfolio Risk process are to determine if:

- Portfolio assumptions (Section 5.1.2.4) are still valid,

- Risk, as assessed, has changed from its prior state with analysis of trends,

- Proper risk management policies and procedures are being followed, and

- Contingency reserves of cost or schedule should be modified in line with the risks.

The Monitor and Control Portfolio Risks process can involve choosing alternative strategies, executing a contingency or fallback plan, taking corrective action, and modifying the portfolio management plan. The risk owner reports periodically to the portfolio manager on the effectiveness of the plan, any unanticipated effects, and any mid-course correction needed to handle the risk appropriately. The Monitor and Control Portfolio Risks process also includes updating the organizational process assets (Section 5.1.1.3), including lessons-learned databases and risk management templates for the benefit of future portfolio activities and projects.

Inputs	Tools & Techniques	Outputs
.1 Portfolio management plan .2 Portfolio risk register .3 Component progress reports .4 Component data	.1 Portfolio risk audits .2 Variance and trend analysis .3 Status meetings .4 Portfolio risk reassessment	.1 Portfolio change requests .2 Portfolio risk register updates .3 Organizational process assets

Figure 5-15. Risk Monitoring and Control: Inputs, Tools & Techniques, and Outputs

5.4.1   Monitor and Control Portfolio Risks: Inputs

.1   Portfolio Management Plan

Key components for this input include the assignment of people, time, and other resources to portfolio risk management.

.2   Portfolio Risk Register

The risk register lists identified risks and risk owners, agreed-upon risk responses, specific implementation actions, symptoms and warning signs of risk, residual and secondary risks, a watchlist of low-priority risks, and the time and cost contingency reserves.

.3   Component Progress Reports

Component managers provide periodic reports to the portfolio manager of progress with respect to the strategic criteria and key performance indicators. The component manager will need to explain any significant variance from the planned performance and, whenever possible, propose corrective actions.

.4   Component Data

Information on the progress, deliverables, and closure of components provides information on work performance that may influence the risk management processes.

5.4.2 Monitor and Control Portfolio Risks: Tools and Techniques

.1 Portfolio Risk Audits

Risk audits examine and document the effectiveness of risk responses in dealing with identified risks and their root causes, as well as the effectiveness of the risk management process.

.2 Variance and Trend Analysis

The portfolio manager should review trends in the portfolio's execution using performance data. Outcomes from these analyses may help forecast potential longer-term deviation of the portfolio from strategic targets. Deviation from the baseline plan may indicate the potential impact of threats or opportunities. Trends are also useful for evaluating the effectiveness of earlier response actions.

.3 Status Meetings

Portfolio risk management should be an agenda item at periodic status meetings. The duration of the discussion may vary depending on the risks that have been identified, their priority, and difficulty of response.

.4 Portfolio Risk Reassessment

The Monitor and Control Portfolio Risk process often requires identification of new risks and analysis and response planning, using the other processes of this chapter as appropriate. Portfolio risk reassessments should be scheduled either at fixed periods or in conjunction with specific events in the project life cycle. The amount and detail of repetition that is appropriate depends on how the portfolio progresses relative to its objectives. For instance, if a risk emerges that was not anticipated in the risk register or included on the watchlist, or if its impact on objectives is different from what was expected, the planned response may not be adequate. It will then be necessary to perform additional response planning to control the risk.

5.4.3 Monitor and Control Portfolio Risks: Outputs

.1 Portfolio Change Requests

Implementing contingency plans or workarounds frequently results in a requirement to change the portfolio management plan to respond to risks. If approved, the portfolio manager integrates these changes into the portfolio management plan for execution with its associated Monitor and Control Portfolio Risks process.

.2 Portfolio Risk Register Updates

An updated risk register contains:

- **Outcomes of risk reassessments, risk audits, and periodic risk reviews.** These outcomes may include updates to probability, impact, priority, response plans, ownership, and other elements of the risk register. Outcomes can also include closure of risks that are no longer applicable. The portfolio manager can integrate this information into the portfolio status reports generated by the Review and Report Portfolio Performance process (Section 4.9).

- **A record of the portfolio's risks and risk responses.** The portfolio/component managers should record the actual outcomes of the portfolio's risks and risk responses. This can help managers plan for risk on future portfolio components as well as elsewhere in the organization.

.3 Organizational Process Assets

The four Portfolio Risk Management processes produce information that can be used later in managing the portfolio, and this information should be captured in the inventory of organizational process assets. Lessons learned from the portfolio risk management activities can contribute to the lessons learned knowledge database of the organization. This information should include data on the actual impact of the risks on strategic objectives and the effectiveness of specific responses.

SECTION IV

APPENDICES

Appendix A

- Second Edition Changes

Appendix B

- Development of *The Standard for Portfolio Management*

Appendix C

- Contributors and Reviewers of *The Standard for Portfolio Management* – Second Edition

APPENDIX A

SECOND EDITION CHANGES

The purpose of this appendix is to give a detailed explanation of the changes made to *The Standard for Portfolio Management*, to develop *The Standard for Portfolio Management* – Second Edition.

A.1 Structural Changes

There are some dramatic revisions to *The Standard for Portfolio Management* – Second Edition. There is also a marked difference in structure. *The Standard for Portfolio Management* – Second Edition is structured to integrate the addition of Knowledge Areas for Portfolio Management, which previously were not part of *The Standard for Portfolio Management*, as described in the side-by-side comparison of distinctions in Table A1.

Table A1. Structural Changes

Original 2006 Edition	2008 Revision
Section I—The Portfolio Management Framework Chapters 1 and 2	Section I—The Portfolio Management Framework Chapters 1 and 2
Section II—The Standard for Portfolio Management Chapter 3 Portfolio Management Processes	Section II—The Standard for Portfolio Management Chapter 3 Portfolio Management Processes
	Section III—The Portfolio Management Knowledge Areas Chapters 4 and 5
Section III—Appendices Appendix D Tools and Techniques	Section IV—Appendices
Section IV—Glossary and Index	Section V—Glossary and Index

A.1.1 Addition of Knowledge Areas

In *The Standard for Portfolio Management*—Second Edition, two Knowledge Areas have been added to map to the two Process Groups. These Knowledge Areas are similar to those of the *PMBOK® Guide*—Fourth Edition Knowledge Areas, however the related inputs, tools and techniques, and outputs in *The Standard for Portfolio Management*—Second Edition are pertinent to the management of portfolios. Therefore, while the *PMBOK® Guide*—Fourth Edition defines the Knowledge Area of Risk Management, the Portfolio Management Knowledge Area is focused appropriately on organizational risk management.

A.1.2 Writing Styles

A style guide was developed and used by the project team to create and finalize the input. Attention was focused on using active voice language and content consistency throughout the document and to provide uniformity with other PMI standards.

A.2 Chapter 1— Introduction Changes

The changes to Chapter 1 describe the fundamental changes to the standard, which has been revised to reflect the standard Knowledge Areas and processes by which portfolio management is widely practiced today. Section 1.1 on Purpose highlights the alignment of this standard with other PMI documents. There is also further discussion on the interactions between project, program, and portfolio management in Chapter 1, and expansion on the portfolio manager's role, knowledge, and skills and the organizational factors involved in portfolio management.

Table A2 summarizes the changes between editions:

Table A2. Chapter 1 Changes

Original 2006 Edition	2008 Revision
1.1 Purpose of *The Standard for Portfolio Management* 1.1.1 Audience for *The Standard for Portfolio Management*	1.1 Purpose of *The Standard for Portfolio Management* 1.1.1 Audience for *The Standard for Portfolio Management*
1.2 What is a Portfolio?	1.2 What is a Portfolio? 1.2.1 The Relationships Among Portfolios, Programs, and Project
1.3 What is Portfolio Management?	1.3 What is Portfolio Management?
1.4 The Link with Organizational Strategy	1.4 The Link between Portfolio Management and Organization Governance
1.5 The Link Between Portfolio Management and Organizational Governance	1.5 The Relationship between Portfolio Management and Organizational Strategy
1.6 The Link Between Portfolio Management and Operations Management 1.6.1 Finance 1.6.2 Marketing 1.6.3 Corporate Communications 1.6.4 Human Resource Management	1.6 The Relationships Among Portfolio, Program, and Project Management
1.7 The Link Between Portfolio Management and Program and Project Management	1.7 The Link between Portfolio Management and Operations Management 1.7.1 The Link between Portfolio Management and Operational Projects 1.7.2 Operational Stakeholders in Portfolio Management

1.8 Role of the Portfolio Manager 1.8.1 Benefits Realization 1.8.2 Program and Project Management Methods and Techniques 1.8.3 Process Development and Continuous Improvement 1.8.4 General Management Skills	1.8 Role of the Portfolio Manager 1.8.1 Strategic Alignment 1.8.2 Portfolio Management Methods and Techniques 1.8.3 Program and Project Management Methods and Techniques 1.8.4 Process Development and Continuous Improvement 1.8.5 General Business Skills 1.8.6 General Management Skills 1.8.7 Stakeholder Management 1.8.8 Risk and Opportunity Management
1.9 Portfolio Management Metrics	1.9 Portfolio Management Reporting and Metrics 1.9.1 Portfolio Reporting and the PMO 1.9.2 Portfolio Management Metrics
1.10 Portfolio Management Reporting 1.10.1 Program/Project Reporting 1.10.2 Financial Reporting	

A.3 Chapter 2—Portfolio Management Overview and Organization

In building a stronger framework between the PMI major standards, incremental detail was added to provide further clarity. Subtle naming differences to clarify Portfolio topics were also incorporated into the revision. Chapter 2 also adds additional stakeholder roles. Section 2.3.4 on Organizational Environmental Factors was added to end the chapter with a discussion of this salient aspect of portfolio management and its importance in organizational influences.

Table A3 summarizes the changes between the editions:

Table A3. Chapter 2 Changes

2006 Edition	2008 Revision
2.1 Portfolio Management Process Overview 2.1.1 Links with Strategy 2.1.2 Portfolio Management Process Cycle	2.1 Portfolio Management Process Overview 2.1.1 Strategy and Investment Alignment 2.1.2 Portfolio Component Management Life Cycle 2.1.3 Portfolio Management Process Cycle 2.1.4 Establishing a Portfolio Management Process
2.2 Portfolio Stakeholder Roles and Responsibilities 2.2.1 Executive Managers 2.2.2 Portfolio Review Board 2.2.3 Portfolio Managers 2.2.4 Sponsors 2.2.5 Program Managers 2.2.6 Project Managers 2.2.7 Program/Project Management Office 2.2.8 Project Team 2.2.9 Operations Management 2.2.10 Functional Managers 2.2.11 Finance Managers 2.2.12 Customers 2.2.13 Vendors/Business Partners	2.2 Portfolio Stakeholder Roles and Responsibilities 2.2.1 Executive Review Board 2.2.2 Portfolio Process Group 2.2.3 Portfolio Management Board 2.2.4 Portfolio Managers 2.2.5 Sponsors 2.2.6 Program Managers 2.2.7 Project Managers 2.2.8 Program/Project Management Office 2.2.9 Project Team 2.2.10 Marketing Management 2.2.11 Operations Management 2.2.12 Engineering Management 2.2.13 Legal Management 2.2.14 Human Resource Management 2.2.15 Functional Managers 2.2.16 Finance Managers 2.2.17 Customers 2.2.18 Vendors/Business Partners
2.3 Organizational Influences 2.3.1 Organizational Culture 2.3.2 Economic Impact 2.3.3 Organizational Impacts	2.3 Organizational Influences 2.3.1 Organizational Culture 2.3.2 Economic Impact 2.3.3 Organizational Impacts 2.3.4 Enterprise Environmental Factors

A.4 Chapter 3—Portfolio Management Processes

Chapter 3 has been revised to map to the Knowledge Areas being introduced in *The Standard for Portfolio Management* – Second Edition. Chapter 3 serves as a standard for managing a portfolio and clearly indicates the two required Portfolio Management Process Groups and their constituent processes. Some of the processes were reshuffled to better flow as portfolio management is practiced.

Table A4 summarizes the changes between the editions:

Table A4. Chapter 3 Changes

2006 Edition	2008 Revision
3.1 Portfolio Management Process Groups 3.1.1 Benefits Management 3.1.2 Stakeholder Management 3.1.3 Portfolio Governance	3.1 Portfolio Management Process Interactions
3.2 Portfolio Management Process Interactions 3.3.1 Aligning Process Group 3.3.2 Monitoring and Controlling Process Group	3.2 Portfolio Management Process Groups
	3.3 Aligning Process Group 3.3.1 Identify Components 3.3.2 Categorize Components 3.3.3 Evaluate Components 3.3.4 Select Components 3.3.5 Identify Portfolio Risks 3.3.6 Analyze Portfolio Risks 3.3.7 Prioritize Components 3.3.8 Develop Portfolio Risk Responses 3.3.9 Balance Portfolio 3.3.10 Communicate Portfolio Adjustment 3.3.11 Authorize Components
	3.4 Monitoring and Controlling Process Group 3.4.1 Monitor and Control Portfolio Risks 3.4.2 Review and Report Portfolio Performance 3.4.3 Monitor Business Strategy Changes

A.5 Chapter 4 and Chapter 5 Changes

Content for Chapters 4 and 5 did not exist in *The Standard for Portfolio Management*. Knowledge Areas have been added and expanded upon, including inputs, tools and techniques, and outputs for each of these areas of portfolio management knowledge:

A.5.1 Chapter 4 Portfolio Governance.

A.5.2 Chapter 5 Portfolio Risk Management.

Tables A5 and A6 summarize the changes between the editions:

Table A5. Chapter 4 Portfolio Governance Changes

2006 Edition	2008 Revision
	4.1 Identify Components
	4.2 Categorize Components
	4.3 Evaluate Components
	4.4 Select Components
	4.5 Prioritize Components
	4.6 Balance Portfolio
	4.7 Communicate Portfolio Adjustment
	4.8 Authorize Components
	4.9 Review and Report Portfolio Performance
	4.10 Monitor Business Strategy Changes

Table A6. Chapter 5 Portfolio Risk Management Changes

2006 Edition	2008 Revision
	5.1 Identify Portfolio Risks
	5.2 Analyze Portfolio Risks
	5.3 Develop Portfolio Risk Responses
	5.4 Monitor and Control Portfolio Risks

A.6 Glossary

The glossary has been expanded and updated to:

- Include those terms within *The Standard for Portfolio Management* – Second Edition that need to be defined to support an understanding of the standard's contents;

- Clarify meaning and improve the quality and accuracy of any translations; and

- Eliminate terms not used within *The Standard for Portfolio Management* – Second Edition.

APPENDIX B

DEVELOPMENT OF *THE STANDARD FOR PORTFOLIO MANAGEMENT*

B.1 Initial Development

B.1.1 Introduction

Since 1996, project managers and organizations have recognized the standard for projects: PMI's *A Guide to the Project Management Body of Knowledge (PMBOK® Guide)*. In 2003, PMI introduced its first standard for organizations called the *Organizational Project Management Maturity Model (OPM3®)*.

Early in 2003, recognizing that the project management profession encompasses a much broader field, including managing multiple projects through programs and portfolios, PMI's Standards Program Team (SPT—which includes the PMI Standards Manager plus the Member Advisory Group) chartered the development of "a standard, or standards," for program management and portfolio management processes.

As in the *PMBOK® Guide* where the standard covers "most projects most of the time," the charter for the PPMS Program was to focus on processes that are generally recognized as good practice most of the time. Moreover, the new standard or standards were to emulate the *PMBOK® Guide*—Third Edition, specifically excluding Knowledge Areas as well as tools and techniques. The new standard or standards, however, were to map content relationships to processes and Knowledge Areas described in the *PMBOK® Guide*—Third Edition.

B.1.2 Preliminary Work

In the summer of 2003, the PPMS Team formed, eventually including 416 PMI volunteers representing 36 countries under the leadership of David Ross, Project Manager, and Paul Shaltry, Deputy Project Manager.

One of the first challenges was the need to establish common agreement on the key definitions, in this case, "program," "program management," "portfolio," and "portfolio management." The PMI Standards Manager brought together all of the active standards teams to achieve consensus on these definitions. The team leaders agreed on common definitions to be included in the *PMBOK® Guide*—Third Edition and this formed the foundation for the program and portfolio management standards.

Next, the PPMS Team looked at whether the two subjects should be combined as one standard or treated separately. A subteam was formed to perform a literature survey and poll the PM community to determine the differences and similarities between program and portfolio management processes. The research confirmed that while program management processes provide for the management of a group of interdependent projects, portfolio management comprises continuous, repeatable, and sustainable processes designed to map business requirements and objectives to projects and programs. As a result of this investigation, the PPMS Team concluded that the profession would be best served with two standards.

Despite the differences in these processes, the PPMS Team believed that because of the relationships between the two subjects and that these were first time standards, it would be best to manage them both under one program. The PPMS Core Team proposed this approach to the SPT, which approved the recommendation. In kind, the PPMS Team developed detailed requirements for each standard that the SPT also approved. The Core Team developed a program plan and general team orientation, which was mandatory, to help volunteers engage effectively. Development of both standards began in early 2004.

B.1.3 Drafting *The Standard for Portfolio Management*

The Portfolio Management Architecture Team (PortMAT), which comprised 13 participants, led first by Larry Goldsmith and then jointly by Beth Ouellette and Claude Emond, organized into three subteams: Content, Process, and Governance. While most of the work was done virtually, the team gathered for a breakthrough meeting in Montreal in July 2004. There, the team was able to focus on the processes of portfolio management and how they interconnect.

The group had much debate as to whether the proposed standard should include the introduction of a portfolio management system to an organization or whether it should focus purely on the ongoing processes of portfolio management. The team agreed that the proposed processes had to assume that the portfolio had already been established within the organization.

Between July and September, the PortMAT conducted a series of team reviews and feedback sessions to connect the related processes. The team met again in Montreal to put the finishing touches on the first complete draft prior to handing it off to the Edit and Quality Teams in late September.

In the last quarter of 2004, the PortMAT's draft standard underwent separate reviews by the PPMS Edit and Quality Teams in preparation for a broader review by, potentially, the whole PPMS Team. This broader review emulated the eventual global exposure draft review that PMI would conduct. This "pre-exposure draft" process generated 950 comments from PPMS volunteers around the worlds.

The PortMAT's work benefited from these comments and recommendation in the improvement or confirmation of content, even though a significant number of comments received were editorial. In general, this internal exposure draft process validated that the PortMAT's draft was on target, as reviewers did not identify any major gaps.

B.1.4 Delivering *The Standard for Portfolio Management*

The PPMS Core Team guided the final revisions and submitted the revised version to the general PPMS Team for a consensus vote. The overwhelming majority of those voting indicated acceptance of the proposed standard without reservation. The Core Team approved the proposed standard before turning it over to the SPT for review and approval in February 2005. The SPT engaged independent subject matter experts to augment the review process. From there, minor refinements were made and the proposed standard was submitted to a 90-day Exposure Draft process starting in May.

The exposure draft period for the *Standard for Portfolio Management* ended on July 9. PMI received 455 comments that the PPMS Adjudication Team reviewed. More than half of these comments were accepted, accepted with modification, or identified for review in the next version of the standard. The PPMS Core Team approved the actions of the Adjudication Team and directed the final edit and approval of the proposed. Only one adjudication action was appealed, and PMI's Adjudication Appeals Team subsequently resolved it.

In October 2005, the PPMS Core Team submitted the final draft for approval by the PMI Standards Consensus Team and subsequent publication.

B.1.5 *The Standard for Portfolio Management* Project Core Team

The following individuals served as members, were contributors of text or concepts, and served as leaders within the Project Core Team (PCT):

David W. Ross, PMP, Project Manager	Paul E. Shaltry, PMP, Deputy Project Manager	
Claude Emond, MBA, PMP	Larry Goldsmith, MBA, PMP	Nancy Hildebrand, BSc, PMP
Jerry Manas, PMP	Patricia G. Mulcair, PMP	Beth Ouellette, PMP
Tom E. Vanderheiden, PMP	Clarese Walker, PMP	David Whelbourn, MBA, PMP
Michael A. Yinger		

B.1.6 Significant Contributors

In addition to the members of the Project Core Team, the following individuals provided significant input or concepts:

Greg Alexander, PhD, PE	Ronald L. Anderson, PMP, MPM	A. Kent Bettisworth
Mark E. Bouska, PMP	Peggy J. Brady, PMP	Lisa Clark
Nancy A. Cygan, PMP	Jeffrey J. Dworkin, PMP	Polisetty Veera Subrahmanya Kumar, PMP
Robert LaRoche, PMP	Angela Lummel, PMP	Russell McDowell, M. Eng., PMP
Graham McHardy	Laura L. Miller, PMP	Crispin (Kik) Piney, PMP
Clare J. Settle, PMP	Thomas Walenta, PMP	Thomas Williamson, PMP

B.1.7 *The Standard for Portfolio Management Project* Team Members

In addition to those listed above, the following Portfolio Management Team Members provided input to and recommendations on drafts of *The Standard for Portfolio Management*:

Mohamed Hosney Abdelgelil	Fred Abrams, PMP, CPL
Pankaj Agrawal, PMP, CISA	Eduardo O. Aguilo, PMP
Zubair Ahmed, PMP	Mounir A. Ajam, MS, PMP
Joyce Alexander	Petya Alexandrova, PMP
Shelley M. Alton, MBA, PMP	Luis E. Alvarez Dionisi, MS, PMP
Neelu Amber	Cynthia Anderson, PMP
Mauricio Andrade, PMP	Jayant Aphale, PhD, MBA
Michael Appleton, CMC, PMP	V. Alberto Araujo, MBA, PMP
Jose Carlos Arce Rioboo, PMP	Alexey O. Arefiev, PMP
Mario Arlt, PMP	Julie Arnold, PMP
Canan Z. Aydemir	Darwyn S. Azzinaro, PMP
AC Fred Baker, PMP, MBA	Rod Baker, MAPM, CPM
Lorie A. Ballbach, PMP	Harold Wayne Balsinger
Keith E. Bandt, PMP	Kate Bankston, PMP
Anil Bansal	Christina Barbosa, PMP
John P. Benfield, PMP	Randy Bennett, PMP, RCC
David D. Bigness, Jr.	Susan S. Bivins, PMP
Jeroen Bolluijt	Dave M. Bond, PhD, PMP
Stephen F. Bonk, PMP, PE	Herbert Borchardt, PMP
Ann Abigail Bosacker, PMP	Christine M. Boudreau
Laurent Bour, PMP	Lynda Bourne, DPM, PMP
Sonia Boutari, PMP	David Bradford, PMP
Adrienne L. Bransky, PMP	Donna Brighton, PMP
Shirley F. Buchanan, PMP	Matthew Burrows, MIMC, PMP
Jacques Cantin	James D. Carlin, PMP
Margareth F. Santos Carneiro, PMP, MsC	Brian R. Carter, PMP
Jose M. Carvalho, PMP	Pietro Casanova, PMP
Trevor Chappell, FIEE, PMP	Gordon Chastain
Deepak Chauhan, PMP, APM	Eshan S. Chawla, MBA, PMP
Keith Chiavetta	Jaikumar R. Chinnakonda, PMP
Edmond Choi	Sandra Ciccolallo

Kurt J. Clemente Sr., PMP

April M. Cox, PMP

Margery J. Cruise, MSc, PMP

Kiran M. Dasgupta, MBA, PMP

Kenneth M. Daugherty, PMP

Pallab K. Deb, B Tech, MBA

D. James Dickson, PMP

Peter Dimov, PMP, CBM

Janet Dixon, PMP, EdD

Anna Dopico, PMP

Karthik Duddala

Karen K. Dunlap, PMP, SSGB

Lowell D. Dye, PMP

Daniella Eilers

Michael T. Enea, PMP, CISSP

Clifton D. Fauntroy

Ezequiel Ferraz, PMP

Joyce M. Flavin, PMP

Robert J. Forster, MCPM, PMP

Serena E. Frank, PMP

Lorie Gibbons, PMP

John Glander

Victor Edward Gomes, BSc, PMP

Mike Goodman, PMP, MSEE

Alicia Maria Granados

Steve Gress, PMP

Yvonne D. Grymes

Papiya Gupta

Deng Hao

Holly Hickman

MD Hudon, PMP

Harold S. Hunt, PMP

Isao Indo, PMP, PE, JP

Suhail Iqbal, PE, PMP

Venkata Rao Jammi, MBA, PMP

Jose Correia Alberto, MSc, LCGI

Mark R. Cox, PMP

Damyan Georgiev Damyanov

Sushovan Datta

Stephanie E. Dawson, PMP

Nikunj Desai

Christopher DiFilippo, PMP

Vivek Dixit

Ross Domnik, PMP

Jim C. Dotson, PMP

Renee De Mond

Charles A. Dutton, PMP

Barbara S. Ebner

Michael G. Elliott

Michael P. Ervick, MBA, PMP

Linda A. Fernandez, MBA

Maviese A. Fisher, PMP, IMBA

Jacqueline Flores, PMP

Carolyn A. Francis, PMP

Kenneth Fung, PMP, MBA

Lisa Ann Giles, PMP

Sunil Kumar Goel, PMP

Andres H. Gonzalez D. ChE

Ferdousi J. Gramling

Bjoern Greiff, PMP

Naveen Grover

Claude L. Guertin, BSc, PMP

Bulent E. Guzel, PMP

Cheryl Harris-Barney

David A. Hillson, PhD, PMP

Sandy Yiu Fai Hui

Zeeshan Idrees, BSc

Andrea Innocenti, PMP

Anshoom Jain, PMP

David B. Janda

Haydar Jawad, PMP

Monique Jn-Marie, PMP

Martin H. Kaerner, PhD, Ing

Kenday Samuel Kamara

Malle Kancherla, PMP

Saravanan Nanjan Kannan, PMP

Ashish Kemkar, PMP

Todd M. Kent, PMP

Sandeep Khanna, MBA, PMP

Raymond R. Klosek, PMP

Mary M. Kosovich, PMP, PE

Koushik Sudeendra, PMP

S V R Madhu Kumar, MBA, PMP

Girish Kurwalkar, PMP

Puneet Kuthiala, PMP

Guilherme Ponce de Leon S. Lago, PMP

Terry Laughlin, PMP

Ade Lewandowski

Jeffrey M. Lewman, PMP

Giri V. Lingamarla, PMP

J. Kendall Lott, PMP

Susan MacAndrew, MBA, PMP

Saji Madapat, PMP, CSSMBB

Subbaraya N. Mandya, PMP

Tony Maramara

Franck L. Marle, PhD, PMP

Dean R. Mayer

Philippe Mayrand, PMP

Amy McCarthy

Eric McCleaf, PMP

Christopher F. McLoon

David McPeters, PMP

Vladimir I. Melnik, MSc, PMP

M. Aslam Mirza, MBA, PMP

Nahid Mohammadi, MS

G. Lynne Jeffries, PMP

Kenneth L. Jones, Jr., PMP

Craig L. Kalsa, PMP

Michael Kamel, PEng, PMP

Soundaian Kamalakannan

Barbara Karten, PMP

Geoffrey L. Kent, PMP

Thomas C. Keuten, PMP, CMC

Karu Godwin Kirijath

Richard M. Knaster, PMP

Victoria Kosuda

Narayan Krish, PMP, MS

Puneet Kumar

Janet Kuster, PMP, MBA

Olaronke Arike Ladipo, MD

David W. Larsen, PMP

Fernando Ledesma, PM, MBA

Corazon B. Lewis, PMP

Lynne C. Limpert, PMP

Cheryl D. Logan, PMP

Dinah Lucre

Douglas Mackey, PMP

Erica Dawn Main

Ammar W. Mango, PMP, CSSBB

Hal Markowitz

Sandeep Mathur, PMP, MPD

Warren V. Mayo, PMP, CSSBB

Yves Mboda, PMP

Richard C. McClarty, Sr.

Malcolm McFarlane

Kevin Patrick McNalley, PMP

Carl J. McPhail, PMP

Philip R. Mileham

Rahul Mishra

Sandhya Mohanraj, PMP

Subrata Mondal

Balu Moothedath

Sharon D. Morgan-Redmond, PMP

Dr. Ralf Muller, PMP

Praveen Chand Mullacherry, PMP

Sreenikumar G. Nair

Carlos Roberto Naranjo P., PMP

Sean O'Neill, PMP

Rolf A. Oswald, PMP

Sukanta Kumar Padhi, PMP

Anil Peer, P.Eng., PMP

Zafeiris K. Petalas PhD Candidate

D. Michele Pitman

Todd Porter

Yves Pszenica, PMP

Peter Quinnell, MBA

Madhubala Rajagopal, MCA, PMP

Sameer S. Ramchandani, PMP

Raju N. Rao, PMP, SCPM

Carolyn S. Reid, PMP, MBA

Bill Rini, PMP

Cynthia Roberts

Allan S. Rodger, PMP

Dennis M. Rose, PMP

Julie Rundgren

Gunes Sahillioglu, MSc, MAPM

Mansi A. Sanap

Kulasekaran C. Satagopan, PMP, CQM

John Schmitt, PMP

Mark N. Scott

Sunita Sekhar, PMP

Nandan Shah, PMP

Donna-Mae Shyduik

Arun Singh, PMP, CSQA

Anand Sinha

Donald James Moore

Roy E. Morgan, PE, PMP

Saradhi Motamarri, MTech, PMP

Seetharam Mukkavilli, PhD, PMP

Kannan Sami Nadar, PMP

Vinod B. Nair, BTech, MBA

Nigel Oliveira, PMP, BBA

Bradford Orcutt, PMP

Louis R. Pack, PMP

Lennox A. Parkins, MBA, PMP

Sameer K. Penakalapati, PMP

Susan Philipose

Charles M. Poplos, EdD, PMP

Ranganath Prabhu, PMP

Sridhar Pydah, PMP

Sueli S. Rabaca, PMP

Mahalingam Ramamoorthi, PMP

Prem G. Ranganath, PMP, CSQE

Tony Raymond, PMP

Geoff Reiss, FAPM, MPhil

Steven F. Ritter, PMP

Andrew C. Robison, PMP

Randy T. Rohovit

Jackson Rovina, PMP

Diana Russo, PMP

Banmeet Kaur Saluja, PMP

Nandakumar Sankaran

Gary Scherling, PMP, ITIL

Neils (Chris) Schmitt

Stephen F. Seay, PMP

David Seto, PMP

Shoukat M. Sheikh

Derry Simmel, PMP, MBA

Deepak Singh, PMP

Ron Sklaver, PMP, CISA

Michael I. Slansky, PMP

Christopher Sloan

Noel Smyth

Keith J. Spacek

Srinivasan Govindarajulu, PMP

Marie Sterling, PMP

Curtis A. Stock, PMP

LeConte F. Stover, MBA, PMP

Juergen Sturany, PMP

Mohammed Suheel, BE, MCP

Vijay Suryanarayana, PMP

Alexander M. Tait

Ali Taleb, MBA, PMP

Sai K. Thallam, PMP

James M. Toney, Jr.

Jonathan Topp

Shi-Ja Sophie Tseng, PMP

Ian Turnbull

U. S. Srikanth, MS, PMP

Nageswaran Vaidyanathan, PMP

Thierry Vanden Broeck, PMP

Paula Ximena Varas, PMP

Alberto Villa, PMP, MBA

Namita Wadhwa, CAPM

Yongjiang Wang, PMP

Kevin R. Wegryn, PMP, MA

Rick Woods, MBA, PMP

Cai Ding Zheng, PMP

Leon Zilber, MSc, PMP

Nancy A. Slater, MBA, PMP

Dennis M. Smith

Jamie B. Solak, MAEd

Gomathy Srinivasan, PMP

Joyce Statz, PhD, PMP

Martin B. Stivers, PMP

Michael E. Stockwell

Anthony P. Strande

Kalayani Subramanyan, PMP

Patricia Sullivan-Taylor, MPA, PMP

Dawn C. Sutherland, PMP

Martin D. Talbott, PMP

David E. Taylor, PMP

Ignatius Thomas, PMP

Eugenio R. Tonin, PMP

T.S. Murthy, PMP

Yen K. Tu

M. Ulagaraj, PhD

Marianne Utendorf, PMP

Ernest C. Valle, MBA, PMP

Gary van Eck, PMP

Jayadeep A. Vijayan, BTech, MBA

Ludmila Volkovich

Jane B. Walton, CPA

Michael Jeffrey Watson

Richard A. Weller, PMP

Fan Wu

Yuchen Zhu, PMP

B.1.8 Final Exposure Draft Reviewers and Contributors

In addition to team members, the following individuals provided recommendations for improving *The Standard for Portfolio Management*:

Hussain Ali Al-Ansari, Eur Ing, C Eng	Mohammed Abdulla Al-Kuwari, PMP, C Eng	Mohammed Safi Batley, MIM
Dennis Bolles, PMP	JoAnn Bujarski	Rachel A. Ciliberti, PMP
Kathleen M. Clore, PMP	Aaron Coffman, PMP	John E. Cormier, PMP
Wanda Curlee, PMP	Serena Frank, PMP	Stanislaw Gasik
Michael F. Hanford	Dr. Robert Hierholtz, PMP, MBA	Kenji Hiraishi, PMP
Charles L. Hunt	Grant Jefferson, PMP	Glen Maxfield, MBA, PMP
Kazuhiko Okubo, PMP, PE	Robert E. Perrine, PMP, ITIL-SM	Crispin (Kik) Piney, PMP
Mitch Provost, PMP	Bernard Roduit	Chandrashekar Satyanarayana, PMP
Margaret H.M. Schaeken, PMP, Hon BSc Math	Marty Sheets, MBA, PMP	Kazuo Shimizu, PMP
Larry Sieck	Leigh M. Stewart, MBA, PMP	Sander Stoffels
George Sukumar	Masanori Takahashi, PMP	Massimo Torre, PhD, PMP
David Violette, PMP	Patrick Weaver, PMP FAICD	Rebecca A. Winston, Esq
Ian M.C. Wolfe, MPM, PMP		

B.1.9 PMI Standards Member Advisory Group (MAG)

The following individuals served as members of the PMI Standards Program Member Advisory Group during development of *The Standard for Portfolio Management*:

Julia M. Bednar, PMP	Carol Holliday, PMP	Thomas Kurihara
Debbie O'Bray	Asbjorn Rolstadas, PhD	Cyndi Stackpole, PMP
Bobbye Underwood, PMP	Dave Violette, MPM, PMP	

B.1.10 Production Staff

Special mention is due to the following employees of PMI:

Ruth Anne Guerrero, PMP, Standards Manager

Dottie Nichols, PMP, Former Standards Manager

Kristin L. Vitello, Standards Project Specialist

Nan Wolfslayer, Standards Project Specialist

Dan Goldfischer, Editor-in-Chief

Richard E. Schwartz, Product Editor

Barbara Walsh, Publications Planner

B.2 *The Standard for Portfolio Management*—Second Edition

B.2.1 Introduction

In 2005, PMI introduced *The Standard for Portfolio Management.* In 2006, a project team was formed and tasked with updating and enhancing Chapters 1 through 3 of the standard. More specifically, the team's charter was to review, validate, or update *The Standard for Portfolio Management* by:

- Ensuring the standard is reviewed and harmonized with the *The Standard for Program Management* – Second Edition, *A Guide to the Project Management Body of Knowledge* (*PMBOK® Guide*) – Fourth Edition, and *OPM3®* – Second Edition.

- Reviewing all material, comments, and feedback relevant to Chapters 1 through 3 and the glossaries developed during the development of *The Standard for Portfolio Management,* determining whether the material will be included in the new edition, and tracking the disposition.

- Developing Knowledge Areas for *The Standard for Portfolio Management* – Second Edition*.*

- Reviewing all text and graphics in the standard to make sure the information is clear, complete and relevant, revising as necessary.

B.2.2 Preliminary Work

In September 2006, the PPMS Team formed, eventually including 167 PMI volunteers representing 35 countries under the leadership of Larry Goldsmith, Project Manager, and Maria Hondros, Deputy Project Manager.

A key tenet for the Second Edition was to harmonize with three other primary standards documents. Along with a PMI-assigned Project Manager, the represented Standards Project Managers and Deputy Project Managers formed a steering committee to support harmonization activities.

B.2.3 Drafting *The Standard for Portfolio Management* – Second Edition

The Portfolio Management Standard Second Edition Leadership Team (PortMAT), which comprised seven participants, was organized into five subteams: Content, Integration, Editorial, Quality, and Communications.

B.2.4   Forming

The call for volunteers went out in December 2006 and the subteam leads worked diligently to assemble their participants. Our Communications Lead, Jean Kelm, worked tirelessly with the subteam leads to identify potential team candidates and finalize the working subteams. The goal was to create global multi-cultural teams to ensure that the finished product would be reflective of our audience. We had so many volunteers that we could not accommodate them all in an active role and therefore a large portion were asked to assume a role as content reviewers.

B.2.5   Developing Content

The first step was to create and gain acceptance of how the content map would change for the second edition. The Content subteam, led by Mark Bouska, formulated a proposed content map. This map was then confirmed with the standard governance chain and validated through two standards working sessions, conducted in coordination with PMI Global congresses in North America (November 2006), Asia Pacific (Jan 2007) and EMEA (May 2007) regions. Once approved and validated, the content subteam created chapter teams to expand the standard. In March 2007, the development of the second edition was well underway. The team met in San Diego in August 2007 to put the finishing touches on the first complete draft prior to handing it off to the Edit Team, led by Lt. Col. Nan Patton, and Quality Teams, led by Renee Taylor with support from Reha Cimen, in early September. During this time, the team engaged independent subject matter experts to augment the review process. From there, minor refinements were made and the proposed standard went on to a 90-day Exposure Draft process.

B.2.6   Harmonization

One of the most important outcomes for *The Standard for Portfolio Management* – Second Edition was harmonization with the other related major PMI standards. While most of the work was performed virtually, the leadership teams gathered for meetings beginning in Dallas in late September 2006. The key to harmonization was having a team focused on keeping abreast of all the standards under development. Our Integration subteam was enthusiastically led by Alan Shechet.

B.2.7   Wrap-Up

In March 2008, the exposure draft period for *The Standard for Portfolio Management* – Second Edition ended. PMI received 599 recommendations, of which approximately 214 recommendations were editorial. The PPMS Adjudication Team reviewed every recommendation, with more than half accepted, accepted with modification, or identified for review in the next version of the standard. The PortMAT team approved the actions of the Adjudication Team and directed the final edit and approval of the proposed standard. A total of six adjudication actions were appealed, and PMI's adjudication Appeals Team subsequently resolved all of them.

APPENDIX C

CONTRIBUTORS AND REVIEWERS OF *THE STANDARD FOR PORTFOLIO MANAGEMENT* – SECOND EDITION

This appendix lists, alphabetically within groupings, those individuals who have contributed to the development and production of *The Standard for Portfolio Management* – Second Edition. The Project Management Institute is grateful to all of these individuals for their support and acknowledges their contributions to the project management profession.

C.1 *The Standard for Portfolio Management* – Second Edition Project Core Team

The following individuals served as members, were contributors of text or concepts, and served as leaders within the Project Core Team (PCT):

Larry Goldsmith, MBA, PMP, Project Manager

Maria J. Hondros, MBA, PMP, Deputy Project Manager

Mark E. Bouska, PMP

Jean M. Kelm, PMP, CAMS

Nanette S. Patton, MSHRM, MSBA

Allan Shechet, MAOD, PMP

Renee Taylor, PMP

M. Elaine Lazar, MA, MA, Project Specialist

C.2 Significant Contributors

In addition to the members of the Project Core Team, the following individuals provided significant input or concepts:

Jennifer A. Arndt, PMP, PgMP

John P. Benfield, PMP, SSBB

Reha Cimen, PMP, MBA

Joseph Fehrenbach, PMP, MBA

Marian "Sami" Hall, PMP

Ruth Houser, PMP

Sarma Kompalli, PMP

Graham McHardy

David Morgen, MBA, PMP

Laurence Moss

Roger P. Neeland, PhD, PMP

Crispin ("Kik") Piney, BSc, PMP

Joshua R. Poulson, PMP

Ing. Biagio Tramontana, PMP

Ron Sklaver

Thomas Williamson, PMP, SCPM

C.3 *The Standard for Portfolio Management* – Second Edition Project Team Members

In addition to those listed above, the following Program Management team members provided input to and recommendations on drafts of *The Standard for Portfolio Management* –Second Edition:

Nada Abandah

Panayotis Agrapidis, MSc CEng

Rania Al-Maghraby, PMP, MSc

Jose Carlos Arce Rioboo, PMP, MBA

Raviendran Arunasalem, PMP

Eng. Dimah M. Barakat, PMP

Daniel J. Barnardo

Murali K. Bharat, PMP

Eric D. Brown, MBA, PMP

John E. Buxton, PMP

Trevor Chappell, EurIng, FIET

Noman Zafar Chaudry, PE, PMP

Daniel R. Crissman, MBA

William H. Dannenmaier, MBA, PMP

Elizabeth Borges, PMP

Karen K. Dunlap, PMP, SSGB

Michael D. Farley, MBA, PMP

Claudio Fernando Freita

Anton Dantrell Gates

Mohamed Gouda Gebriel

Robert Goodhand, PMP

Evgenii Gromakov, PhD

Hideyuki Hikida, PMP

Brian Irwin, MSM, PMP

Srinivas Adusumilli, PMP

Fathalla M. Al-Hanbali, PMP

Guna Appalaraju

Mario Arlt, PMP

Dennis G. Ballow, Sr., PMP, MAEd

Nathaniel Barksdale, Jr., PhD, PMP

Kenneth J. Barry

Michael F. Blankenstein, MS, PMP

Jim Burkholder, PMP, CSSBB

Kamaljeet K. Cato

Mubarak A. Chaudry

Rajasekhar Chevvuri, PMP

Anthony J Cunningham, PMP, MSIS

Jean-Michel De Jaeger, EMBA, PMP

Natalia Dimu, PMP

Hassan El-Meligy

Paulo A. Ferreira, PMP

Steve Garfein, MBA, PMP

Yohan Gaumont

Peter Glynne, MPM

Shyam Kumar Gopinathan Nair, PMP

Sandra Herrmann

Brigitte Hoffmann, MBA, PMP

Leon Jackson Jr., PMP, FEA

Swatee Jain

Hemant Julka

Paul Karlzen, PMP, JD

Harlan G. Kennedy, PEng, PMP

Adil O. Khan, PMP

Daniel Kim

Wendy Kraly, PMP, MBA

Sanjeeva Kuma

Joe LaGrua, PMP, MIS

Rosalie Lalena

Marcelo La Roza

John Lissaman, BEng, PMP

Venu G Madduri, MBA, PMP

Prashant Malviya, PMP

Greg Martin, PhD, PMP

Tim Massie, PgMP, PMP

Charmaine McKernan

Pauline P. Meilleur

Laura Metzger

Myles D. Miller, PMP, MBA

Lincoln Sant'Ana Morales, PMP

Nanduri V. Rao, PMP

Elena Navas

David R. Nunn, MBA, PMP

Molli Ong

Sathyanarayanan Pandalai, PMP, CISA

Heidi Brakke Peterson, PMP

Hari Pisati, MBA, PMP

Richard Price

Renato Putini, MBA

Saifur Rehman, PMP, PE

Ramon Jimenez, PMP

Chin-Chi Kao

Tomer Keidar

Rameshchandra B. Ketharaju, CSQA

Khalid Ahmad Khan, PE, PMP

Sudeendra Koushik, PMP

Meeta Kumar, PMP, MBA

Lisa J. LaBonte, PMP

Rupendra Mohan Lahoti, PMP

Morgan J. Langley, PMP

Nealand M. Lewis, MBA, PMP

Rodrigo Loureiro, PMP

Vishal Maheshwari, MBA, PMP

Narendra Marikale, PMP

Steven B. Martin, PMP

Laura Mazzaferro, PMP

Richard J. Meertens, PMP, MBA

Geeta Menon, PMP

Stalin Michael, MS, MBA

Beverley Miranda, MBA, PMP

Belatchew (Abby) Nadew, PMP

Carlos Naranjo, PMP

Nyanisi Joseph Nhlapo

Edgar Méndez Ocádiz, PMP

Rebecca S. Overcash, MBA, PMP

Shiri R. Persaud, PMP

Tonya M. Peterson, PMP, MSPM

Tracy Poon, PMP, MBA

Brian Pubrat, PMP

Elena Ramírez Márquez

Marlene Derian Robertson, PMP

Virginia Oliva Rodriguez

Angela M. Ruthenberg, PMP

Saleh Sailik, PMP, PMOC

Neel Shah, BBA, MIB

Angela P. Scott, PMP

Prakash Ramesh Sharma, MBB, PMP

Vivek Sivakumar, CAPM

Lavine Oscene Small

V.S.Srividhya, PMP, MCA

Gangesh Thakur, CPIM, PMP

Fuminori Toyama

Venu Uppalapati, PMP

Marconi Fabio Vieira, PMP

Colin D. Watson, MIEE, PMP

Lai Chi Wong, PMP

Rafael Beteli Silva Zanon, PMP

Paula M. K. Zygielszyper, PMP

Bernard Roduit

Ahmed Saleh Bahakim, PMP

Sharad Saxena, PMP

Creg A. Schumann

Dinesh Sharma, PMP, MBA

Shekhar Singh, PMP

Jen L. Skrabak, PMP, MBA

Ulrich Spiehl, MBA

Juergen Sturany, PMP

Julio Toro Silva, MBA, PMP

Prof. S. Tsaltas, MBI, MMath

Ali Vahedi, MSc, PMP

Hao Wang, PMP, PhD

George N. Wolbert, PMP

Joseph M. Zaccaria, PMP

Cristina Zerpa, MC, PMP

C.4 Final Exposure Draft Reviewers and Contributors

In addition to team members, the following individuals provided recommendations for improving *The Standard for Portfolio Management* – Second Edition:

Hussain Ali Al-Ansari, EurIng, CEng

Mohammed Safi Batley, MIM

Dennis G. Ballow, Sr., PMP, MAEd

Lynda Bourne, DPM, PMP

Steve Buschle, PMP

Allan Edward Dean, MBA, PMP

Sheriff Hashem

Hideyuki Hikida, PMP

Zulfiqar Hussain, PE, PMP

Rameshchandra Ketharaju

Henry Kondo, PMP, CISA

Mohammed Abdulla Al-Kuwari, EurIng, PMP

Robert F. Babb II, PMP, PhD

Stephen F. Bonk, PMP, PE

Michael J. Browne, BSc, PhD

Chris Cartwright, MPM, PMP

Stanisław Gasik

Mohamed Hefny

Bernard Hill, PhD, PMP

Tony Johnson

Thomas C. Keuten, PMP, OPM3-CC

Greg Martin, PhD, PMP

Yan Bello Méndez, PMP

Carlos Morais, PMP

Cláudio Barbosa Rodrigues, PMP

Paul E. Shaltry, PMP

Kazuo Shimizu, PMP

Joyce Statz, PhD, PMP

Lisa A. Taylor, PMP, MS

Thierry Verlynde, PMP

Tim Washington

Kevin R. Wegryn, PMP, CPM

Louis J. Mercken, PMI Fellow, PMP

S. Ramani, PgMP, PMP

John Schuyler, PE, PMP

Archana Sharma, PMP, MS

Ron Sklaver, PMP

Michal Szymaczek, PMP

Srikanth U.S., MS, PGCPM

Aloysio Vianna da Silva

Patrick Weaver, PMP, FCIOB

Richard Zoomer

C.5 PMI Standards Member Advisory Group

The following individuals served as members of the PMI Standards Program Member Advisory Group during development of *The Standard for Portfolio Management* – Second Edition:

Julia M. Bednar, PMP

Douglas Clark

Carol Holliday, MA, PMP

Asbjørn Rolstadås, PhD, Ing

Paul E. Shaltry, PMP

Chris Cartwright, MPM, PMP

Terry Cooke-Davies, PhD, FCMI

Debbie O'Bray, CIM (Hons)

David W. Ross, PMP, PgMP

Dave Violette, MPM, PMP

C.6 Staff Contributors

Special mention is due to the following employees of PMI:

Christie Biehl, EdD, PMP, Former Project Manager

Steven L. Fahrenkrog, PMP, VP, Regional Development

Ruth Anne Guerrero, MBA, PMP, Former Standards Manager

Amanda Freitick, Standards Program Administrator

Donn Greenberg, Publications Manager

Roberta Storer, Product Editor

Kristin L. Vitello, Standards Project Specialist

Barbara Walsh, CAPM, Publications Planner

Nancy Wilkinson, MBA, PMP, *OPM3®* Product Specialist

Nan Wolfslayer, AStd, Standards Compliance Specialist

John Zlockie, PMP, Standards Manager

SECTION V

GLOSSARY AND INDEX

Glossary

Index

GLOSSARY

Authorization. The process of approving, funding, and communicating the authorization for initiating work on a component included in the "balanced portfolio."

Business Case. A documented economic feasibility study used to establish validity of the benefits of a selected component lacking sufficient definition and that is used as a basis for the authorization of further project management activities.

Capacity. The resources (human resources, financial, physical assets) which an organization puts at the disposal of portfolio management to select, fund, and execute its components.

Categorization. A grouping of components based on criteria.

Category. A predetermined key description used to group potential and authorized components to facilitate further decision making. Categories usually link their components with a common set of strategic goals.

Class. A key descriptor telling if a (potential) component is a business case, a project, a program, a portfolio, or other work.

Component (Portfolio). A discrete element of a program or a portfolio.

Determining Factors. Key descriptors of the portfolio such as component definition, category definition, key criteria definition, and resources capacity to support the portfolio management process. The determining factors are agreed upon by the executive group and are based on the organization strategic plan.

Effect. Conditional future event or condition which would directly affect one or more portfolio objectives if the associated risk happened.

Evaluation. The process of scoring specific potential components using key indicators and their related weighted criteria for comparison purpose for further decision-making.

Filter. Criteria used to evaluate and select a potential component or decide whether a component meets the "go/no-go" conditions.

Identification. The process of documenting and assembling, for further decision-making, the inventory of ongoing and proposed new components as potential components for categorization.

Impact. A measure of the effect of a risk, if it occurs, on one or more portfolio success criteria. Also known as *consequence*.

Inventory. A set of components, comprising all active components as well as proposals for new components, properly documented using key descriptors, use as a basis for portfolio management decision making.

Key Criteria. Predetermined measures, values, or conditions used in a scoring model to measure alignment with strategic goals.

Key Descriptors. A set of characteristics used to categorize and document a component for further decision-making. It might include among others, specifics about scope, schedule, budget, actual performance (using key performance indicators), class, category, evaluation scores, priority, and approval status.

Key Indicators. A set of parameters that permits visibility into how a component measures up to a given criterion.

Key Performance Indicators. A criterion that permits measurement and reporting.

Management-by-Projects. The application of the project management discipline to achieve or extend an organization's strategic goals.

New Component. A component that is being added to an existing project portfolio.

Organizational Governance. The process by which an organization directs and controls its operational and strategic activities, and by which the organization responds to the legitimate rights, expectations, and desires of its stakeholders.

Other Work. Anything that fits into the "component definition" used by an organization and that cannot be classified as a business case, a project, a program, or a portfolio.

Phase Gates. Decision points to continue, continue with modification, or stop a project, program, or portfolio.

Portfolio. A collection of projects or programs and other work that are grouped together to facilitate effective management of that work to meet strategic business objectives. The projects or programs of the portfolio may not necessarily be interdependent or directly related.

Portfolio Balancing. The process of organizing the prioritized components into a component mix that has the best potential to collectively support and achieve strategic goals.

Portfolio Management. The centralized management of one or more portfolios, which includes identifying, prioritizing, authorizing, managing, and controlling projects, programs and other related work, to achieve specific strategic business objectives.

Portfolio Management Communication Plan. A plan defining all communication needs, establishing communication requirements, specifying frequency, and identifying recipients for information associated with the portfolio management process.

Portfolio Management Life Cycle. A life cycle of processes used to collect, identify, categorize, evaluate, select, prioritize, balance, authorize, and review components within the project portfolio to ensure that they are performing compared with the key indicators and the strategic plan.

Portfolio Management Plan. A document that defines how a portfolio will be organized, monitored, and controlled. It comprises relevant information from the organization's governance rules as well as outputs from the Aligning Process Group, such as the list of portfolio components and their current status, the portfolio risk register, etc.

Portfolio Periodic Reporting and Review. The process of reporting on the portfolio components as a whole using key indicators and reviewing the performance of the component mix by comparing actual with anticipated evolution, value, risk level, spending, and strategic alignment.

Portfolio Risk. An uncertain event, set of events or conditions that, if they occur, have one or more effects, either positive or negative, on at least one strategic business objective of the portfolio.

Potential Component. A component that fits the predetermined "component definition," but has not yet been authorized to be part of the project portfolio.

Prioritization. The process of ranking the selected components based on their evaluation scores and other management considerations.

Program. A group of related projects managed in a coordinated way to obtain benefits and control not available from managing them individually. Programs may include elements of related work outside of the scope of the discrete projects in the program.

Program Management. The centralized coordinated management of a program to achieve the program's strategic objectives and benefits.

Program Management Office. The centralized management of a particular program or programs such that corporate benefit is realized by the sharing of resources, methodologies, tools, and techniques, and related high-level project management focus.

Project. A temporary endeavor undertaken to create a unique product, service, or result.

Project Management. The application of knowledge, skills, tools, and techniques to project activities to meet the project requirements.

Scoring Model. A set of weighted criteria and corresponding key indicators to measure and score components for comparison and prioritization purposes.

Selection. The process of deciding on the components to be put forward from evaluation to prioritization based on their evaluation scores.

Strategic Change. Any change in the strategic intentions and plans of the organization that can impact the contents of component definition, categories, filters, key indicators, and other decision-making parameters used for portfolio management.

Strategic Goals. The definition of an organization's intended achievements in terms of business results interpreted from various perspectives—financial, customer, infrastructure, products and services, or by cultural outcomes that are measurable.

Strategic Plan. A high-level document that explains the organization's vision and mission, plus the approach that will be adopted to achieve this mission and vision, including the specific goals and objectives to be achieved during the period covered by the document.

Subportfolio. A collection of components which includes programs, projects, portfolios, and other work grouped together within a larger portfolio.

Weight. A multiplication factor used to convey the relative importance of key criteria used in a scoring model.

INDEX

A

Adjustment. *See* Communication of portfolio adjustment
Alignment
    Alignment Process Group, 23, 34, 36–37
    portfolio, 10
    strategic, 14, 19, 21, 102
Alignment Process Group, 23, 34, 36–37
Analysis
    asset capacity, 63
    assumptions, 93
    checklist, 93
    communication requirements, 73
    cost benefit, 68, 101
    financial capacity, 62, 98
    graphical methods of, 69
    human resources capacity, 62
    outcome probability, 101
    probability, 69, 101
    quantitative, 68
    risk, 40, 85–86, 88–89, 96–101, 139
    scenario, 68, 104
    sensitivity, 99
    SWOT, 93
    variance and trend analysis, 107
Analyze Portfolio Risks, 40, 96–101
Asset capacity analysis, 63
Assumptions analysis, 93
Audit process, 24
Authorize Components, 22, 24, 42, 49–50, 74–76

B

Balance Portfolio, 41, 49–50, 66–70
    indicators/criteria for, 69
    rebalancing recommendations, 81
Brainstorming, 92
Budget, 72
Business
    processes, 23, 35
    strategy changes, 43, 49, 50, 82–84

C

Capacity data, 78
Categories, 55, 94
Categorize Components, 38, 49–50, 55–56
Cause-and-Effect Diagram, 93–94
Checklist analysis, 93
Communicate Portfolio Adjustment, 41, 49–50, 71–74
Communication requirements analysis, 73
Comparison, 53
Components, 39. *See also* Authorization of components;
    Categorization of components; Evaluation of components
    contributions from, 10
    definition, 51
    identification of, 38, 49
    key descriptors of, 52
    list, 53–54, 60
    prioritization of, 40
    progress reports on, 107
    risk in, 89
Continuous Quality Improvement (CQI), 15
Contributors, 120–125
Cost benefit analysis, 68, 101
CQI. *See* Continuous Quality Improvement
Criteria. *See* Key criteria
Critical resources, 7
Customers, 28

D

Dashboard, 18
Delphi technique, 92
Dependencies, 60
Develop Portfolio Risk Response, 40, 85–86, 89, 102–106,
    139
Diagramming techniques, 94
Diagrams
    cause-and-effect, 93–94
    influence, 94
Directives, 81